EXECUTIVE FUNCTIONING FOR ADULT ADHD SUCCESS

5 Simple Strategies to Master Time Management, Increase Focus, & Enhance Emotional Resilience Without Feeling Overwhelmed or Burned Out

SHARON BANKS

Copyrights

Copyright © 2024 by Sharon Banks

All rights reserved.

No portion of this book may be reproduced in any form without written permission from the publisher or author, except as permitted by U.S. copyright law.

This publication is designed to provide accurate and authoritative information in regard to the subject matter covered. It is sold with the understanding that neither the author nor the publisher is engaged in rendering legal, investment, accounting or other professional services. While the publisher and author have used their best efforts in preparing this book, they make no representations or warranties with respect to the accuracy or completeness of the contents of this book and specifically disclaim any implied warranties of merchantability or fitness for a particular purpose. No warranty may be created or extended by sales representatives or written sales materials. The advice and strategies contained herein may not be suitable for your situation. You should consult with a professional when appropriate. Neither the publisher nor the author shall be liable for any loss of profit or any other commercial damages, including but not limited to special, incidental, consequential, personal, or other damages.

Book Cover by The Cloud Digital

First edition 2024

TABLE OF CONTENTS

Introduction 5

Understanding ADHD and Executive Functioning 9

Strategy #1 23

Strategic Time Management

Strategy #2 40

Enhancing Focus and Productivity

Strategy #3 56

Emotional Intelligence and Resilience

Strategy #4 74

Building and Maintaining Relationships

Strategy #5 88

Lifestyle Adjustments for ADHD Management

Leveraging Technology and Tools 104

Mindset and Emotional Health: Building a Positive ADHD Identity
.... 118

Conclusion 132

References 136

About the Author 142

TABLE OF CONTENTS

Introduction 5

Understanding ADHD and Executive Functioning 9

Strategy #1 23

Strategic Time Management

Strategy #2 40

Enhancing Focus and Productivity

Strategy #3 56

Emotional Intelligence and Resilience

Strategy #4 74

Building and Maintaining Relationships

Strategy #5 88

Lifestyle Adjustments for ADHD Management

Leveraging Technology and Tools 104

Mindset and Emotional Health: Building a Positive ADHD Identity
.... 118

Conclusion 132

References 136

About the Author 142

INTRODUCTION

Have you ever felt like your mind is a browser with too many tabs open, each one vying for your attention, and yet, you can't seem to focus on any of them long enough to make progress? If this sounds familiar, you're not alone. Recent studies show that approximately 10 million adults in the U.S. live with Attention Deficit Hyperactivity Disorder (ADHD). This figure underscores not just prevalence but also the shared challenges in managing daily life with this neurodivergence.

In this book, we probe executive functioning skills, crucial tools for anyone but incredibly transformative for adults with ADHD. These skills, which include managing time, maintaining focus, and regulating emotions, are often the very areas that challenge us the most. Yet, understanding and improving these skills can significantly enhance personal and professional life.

My journey with ADHD has been a winding path of challenges and victories. From struggling with punctuality and deadlines to feeling overwhelmed by emotions, I've experienced the pitfalls of ADHD firsthand. However, I've turned these obstacles into stepping stones for success through dedicated practice and strategic adjustments. This book is a culmination of those personal experiences and practical strategies that I've found effective.

At its core, "Executive Functioning Skills for Adult ADHD Success" aims to shift the narrative from viewing ADHD as a deficit to recognizing it as a difference. This book isn't about overcoming a disorder; it's about embracing your unique cognitive style and leveraging it to your advantage. Each chapter is designed to equip you with knowledge and tools to refine your executive functions, interspersed with anecdotes and backed by the latest research, ensuring you have the inspiration and information needed to thrive.

You can expect a straightforward layout: five chapters dedicated to a specific strategy, from enhancing your time management skills to boosting emotional resilience. These strategies are based on scientific understanding and tested in the fires of personal experience.

This book is for you—the creative thinkers, the round pegs in square holes, the individuals who see the world differently. It's written from a place of deep understanding and solidarity, knowing well the hurdles and the heights of living with adult ADHD. Together, we will explore how to navigate these waters, not by changing who you are, but by understanding and optimizing how you think.

As we embark on this journey together, I am filled with hope. I hope that you will find in these pages the tools you need to manage and excel in your life with ADHD. I hope you will see your incredible potential and the unique strengths that ADHD brings into your life.

Welcome to a new chapter in your story—one where ADHD is not a barrier but a different way of seeing and interacting with the world, ripe with possibilities for innovation and success. Let's begin this journey with open hearts and minds, ready to transform challenges into opportunities for growth and fulfillment.

UNDERSTANDING ADHD AND EXECUTIVE FUNCTIONING

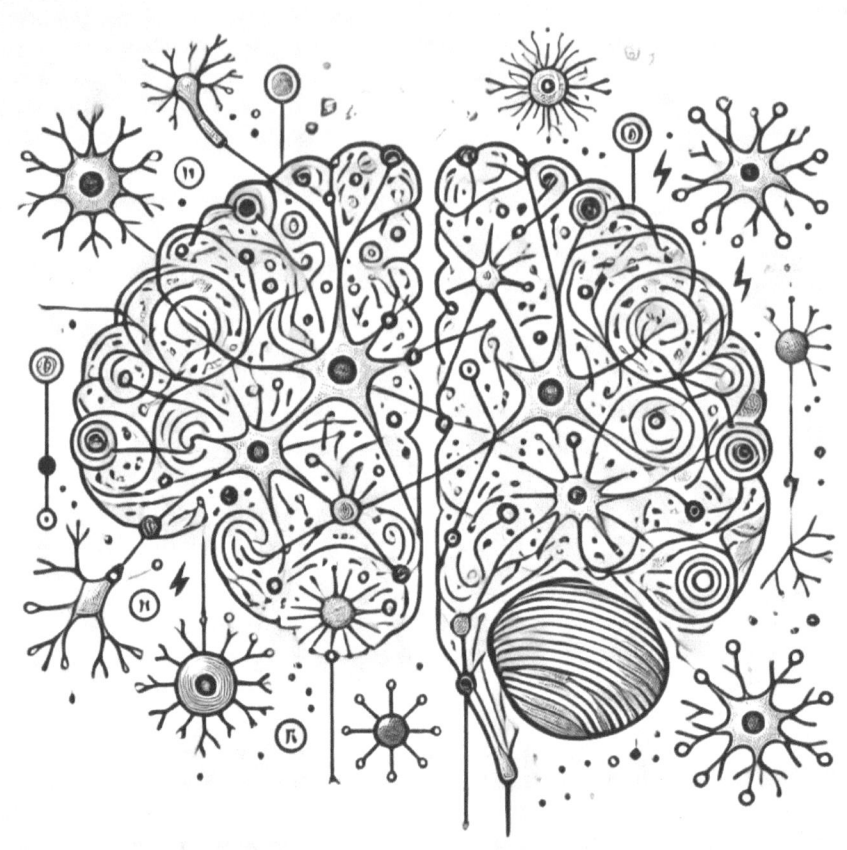

Have you ever had one of those days where nothing went as planned? You start one task, get distracted by another, and feel like you've been busy but accomplished little by the end of the day. It's frustrating, isn't it? For those with ADHD, this scenario might feel like a regular occurrence rather than an occasional mishap. ADHD isn't just about having trouble paying attention. It involves many challenges that affect every aspect of life, from work to personal relationships.

This chapter will explore what ADHD means beyond the typical stereotypes and simple misunderstandings. We'll examine how it impacts your day-to-day functioning and discuss ways to navigate these challenges. By understanding the nuances of ADHD, you can start to see it not just as a series of obstacles but as a different way of interacting with the world that can be managed and even harnessed in beneficial ways.

Decoding ADHD and Its Impact on Daily Functioning

Defining ADHD

Attention Deficit Hyperactivity Disorder (ADHD) is officially classified as a neurodevelopmental disorder, one that significantly impacts the executive functions of the brain, which govern our ability to plan, organize, and regulate our behavior. According to the DSM-5, the diagnostic manual used by mental health professionals, ADHD is characterized by patterns of inattention, hyperactivity, and impulsivity that are inconsistent with the individual's developmental level. This isn't just about occasionally forgetting where you left your keys or feeling restless. It's a pervasive pattern that affects every area of life.

Common Misconceptions

There's a wide array of myths surrounding ADHD that can create stigma and misunderstanding. One common myth is that ADHD only affects children and that it's something you outgrow. This couldn't be further from the truth. ADHD continues into adulthood, and many adults are struggling without ever having been diagnosed as children. Another prevalent misconception is that ADHD is just a lack of discipline, which can lead to judgments that those with ADHD just need to try harder. ADHD has biological roots; it's not a matter of willpower or motivation.

Impact on Daily Tasks

Imagine trying to complete a project with a radio blaring static in the background. That's a day in the life of someone with ADHD. This static makes organizing tasks, prioritizing them, and following through with completion incredibly challenging. For instance, maintaining a calendar might seem simple, but for someone with ADHD, this can feel like a Herculean task. The dynamic nature of managing appointments, remembering deadlines, and planning can often lead to missed dates and frantic last-minute rushes. Completing massive projects can be daunting when focusing on a single task for extended periods feels nearly impossible.

Real-Life Implications

The ripple effects of these challenges in daily tasks go far beyond mere forgetfulness or disorganization. They can strain relationships, where friends and family may not understand why you can't seem to "keep it together." Professionally, the impact can be just as significant, with ADHD individuals often perceived as unreliable or underperformers due to missed deadlines or disorganized workspaces. On a personal level, the constant struggle with seemingly simple tasks can lead to diminished self-esteem and a persistent sense of underachieving despite one's best efforts.

Navigating life with ADHD is not just about battling forgetfulness or distractions. It's about dealing with the misconceptions that come with it, the daily challenges of task management, and the broader implications on your social interactions and self-worth. As we move forward, remember understanding is the first step towards transformation. By redefining ADHD in your terms and recognizing its impact on your life, you're already beginning to take control. In the following sections, we will explore strategies and insights that can help transform these challenges into manageable parts of your life.

The Science of Executive Functions: What They Are and Why They Matter

When we talk about executive functions, we refer to the brain's command center. These cognitive processes help us manage our lives and make decisions. Think of them as orchestra conductors directing and harmonizing our thoughts, actions, and emotions to produce the symphony that is part of our day-to-day lives. These functions include working memory, which allows us to hold and manipulate information at the moment; cognitive flexibility, which is the ability to adapt our thinking to new, unexpected, or complex situations; and inhibitory control, which helps us suppress impulses and distractions that can

...owing about executive functions and how they are affected by ADHD ...vides clarity and empowers us to seek specific strategies that address ...e challenges. By strengthening these skills, you can enhance your ...ity to perform tasks that many find straightforward but can often ...tumbling blocks for those with ADHD. This knowledge is the first ... towards adapting and adopting techniques that can significantly ...rove managing small tasks and the big picture of your life.

...HD and Time Perception: Unwrapping Time Blindness

...e you ever promised to meet someone in five minutes, only to realize ...our has passed once you finally glimpse the clock? This isn't just ...nt-mindedness; for many with ADHD, it's a constant reality known ...**me blindness.** Time blindness is a term used to describe the difficulty ...nderstanding and managing the passage of time. This challenge is ...bout laziness or forgetfulness; it's a fundamental perception issue ...can make minutes feel like hours and hours like minutes.

...roots of time blindness in ADHD are deeply neurological. Inside ...brains, particularly in regions like the prefrontal cortex, neural ...its responsible for gauging time are less active or might function ...rently. This part of the brain is like an orchestra conductor, but for ...one with ADHD, it's as if the conductor is occasionally stepping off ...odium. Without this guidance, our perception of time can become ...ed. Neurotransmitters, such as dopamine, which are involved in ...tion and reward processing, also play a crucial part. In ADHD, ...pamine levels are lower or the receptors are less sensitive, it can ... how time is perceived, making it harder to plan, stay on task, or ...track of deadlines.

...consequences of this altered time perception ripple outwards, ...ing various facets of life. Professionally, it can lead to missed ...ines or chronic delays, which might be mistaken for negligence or ...f commitment. Socially, it can strain relationships; being late can ...n as a sign of disrespect, and no explanation seems to suffice. This ...rception often leads to frustration and embarrassment, further ...ounded by the common misconceptions surrounding ADHD.

derail us from our goals.

Now, let's break down how these parts play out **prefrontal cortex,** located at the front of the brain, is It's responsible for high-level decision-making and When planning what to eat for dinner while finish your prefrontal cortex manages those tasks. Moreove like **dopamine** play a crucial role in this area. Dopa the "feel-good" hormone, but it's also deeply involv motivation. It helps signal the importance of reward you to achieve specific outcomes. However, in dopamine pathways might not function typically, stay focused, follow through on tasks, or manage ti

Linking these executive functions to ADHD, we se with the challenges many adults with ADHD fa working memory is akin to mental juggling, ADH juggling with one hand tied behind your back. It's it's certainly a lot harder. This difficulty can manif such as following a recipe or keeping track of m at work. Cognitive flexibility, or the lack thereof, with adapting to last-minute changes in plans that arise without a clear, preset solution. Whe is compromised, it might lead to impulsive de considering the consequences, whether in a conv even while driving.

Understanding the importance of these functions i be overstated. They are fundamental in helping attention, switch focus, plan and organize, remer inappropriate speaking or behavior. Consider organizing a meeting while managing emails a your team. Effective executive functioning a between these tasks efficiently, prioritize them, and attention across these demands without beco

Navigating life with ADHD can often feel like sa

Given these challenges, mastering time management is crucial. One effective strategy is using external tools like timers or alarms. Setting a timer not only provides a concrete reminder of when to start or stop an activity but also externalizes time, helping to compensate for the internal clock's irregularities. Another helpful approach is time blocking, which divides the day into segments dedicated to specific tasks. This method structures time visually and limits the scope of engagement, making it easier to start and complete tasks. Visual timers, particularly those that show time eluding, can provide a tangible sense of time passing, which is enormously helpful for someone with time blindness.

By acknowledging the underlying neurological components and recognizing the practical implications in daily life, you can begin to adopt tools and techniques that transform these challenges into manageable aspects of your day. These adaptations don't just help stick to schedules; they empower you to navigate life confidently, turning time into an ally rather than an adversary.

Emotional Dysregulation and ADHD: The Hidden Struggle

Emotional dysregulation might not be the first thing that comes to mind when we talk about ADHD, but it's a significant aspect that many of us grapple with daily. So, what exactly is emotional dysregulation? It's a term used to describe difficulties in controlling emotional responses to various situations. For someone with ADHD, this might mean feeling emotions more intensely, having sudden shifts in mood, or struggling to return to a calm state after becoming upset. It's like riding a rollercoaster during extraordinary circumstances, everyday interactions, and tasks, which can be exhausting and bewildering.

The link between emotional dysregulation and ADHD lies deep within our brain's wiring and neurotransmitter activities, particularly involving dopamine and norepinephrine, which affect not only our focus and attention but also our emotions. ADHD often co-exists with an impaired ability to regulate these emotional responses. This impairment can make it challenging to manage the typical ups and downs of life, leading to what many describe as an emotional rollercoaster. For instance, the impulsivity associated with ADHD can cause a person to react hastily to emotional triggers. At the same time, inattention can make recognizing and addressing those emotions challenging before they become overwhelming.

The impact of emotional dysregulation extends far beyond one's internal experience. It can play a significant role in shaping personal and professional relationships. Imagine you're in a work meeting and suddenly feel criticized by a casual remark from a colleague. If you're struggling with emotional dysregulation, your response might be disproportionately intense, perhaps snapping back angrily or visibly upset, which can confuse those around you who might not see the remark as a big deal. These reactions can strain relationships, creating a cycle where misunderstandings and conflicts escalate, leaving feelings of isolation or regret in their wake.

Similarly, emotional dysregulation can lead to volatility in personal relationships. For someone with ADHD, a minor disagreement might quickly escalate into a major conflict. This volatility can be puzzling and exhausting for loved ones who might find the intense emotional reactions disproportionate to the situation. It's not uncommon for these dynamics to lead to patterns of conflict that can be deeply distressing for everyone involved.

Given these challenges, finding effective ways to manage emotional dysregulation is crucial. One of the most effective approaches is mindfulness, which involves practicing awareness of the present moment while calmly acknowledging and accepting one's feelings, thoughts, and bodily sensations. For those of us with ADHD, mindfulness can help slow down the rush of emotions, allowing us to process our feelings more rationally and respond more appropriately. Techniques can include guided meditations, mindful breathing exercises, or even simple practices like pausing to name the emotions you're experiencing throughout the day.

Cognitive-behavioral strategies also offer valuable tools. These involve recognizing the thoughts that trigger emotional responses and learning to reframe them in ways that lead to more balanced emotions. For example, if you interpret offhand remarks as personal criticisms, cognitive-behavioral techniques could help you learn to view such comments more objectively, reducing the emotional impact. This reframing can lessen the intensity and duration of emotional responses, making interactions smoother and reducing the likelihood of conflicts.

Incorporating these techniques into daily life doesn't just help dampen the extremes of emotional dysregulation; it also empowers us to build more stable, understanding, and supportive relationships at work and home. Beyond techniques, knowing this is a shared struggle can lighten the emotional load. Many of us are on this path together, navigating the highs and lows, learning how to find our equilibrium slowly but surely. As we continue this exploration, the strategies and understandings we develop improve our emotional responses and enhance our overall quality of life, making each day a bit more manageable and hopeful.

Cognitive Flexibility in ADHD: Thinking Outside the Box

Cognitive flexibility is like being a mental acrobat; it's about how swiftly and effectively you can shift your thoughts and adapt your behaviors in response to new information, changing conditions, or unexpected obstacles. This ability is crucial when juggling multiple demands, switching between tasks, or solving problems that don't have clear, straightforward solutions. This mental agility allows most people to navigate daily life's unpredictability with relative ease. However, for those of us with ADHD, cognitive flexibility can often feel like a tricky code to crack.

When you live with ADHD, it can sometimes feel as though your brain is wired to have a kind of tunnel vision. This isn't about unwillingness or a lack of effort; it's more about how the neurological makeup of an ADHD brain can limit flexibility. The brain regions involved, particularly the prefrontal cortex, which plays a significant role in managing our thoughts and actions, might not coordinate as smoothly. This can make shifting gears from one activity to another feel as daunting as trying to change the course of a speeding train. It explains why sudden changes in plans can feel jarring or why transitioning from one task to another can be a source of incredible frustration and anxiety.

However, it's not all challenging news. This very aspect of ADHD that makes traditional flexibility difficult also predisposes many of us to a type of divergent thinking that can be a significant asset. Divergent thinking is the ability to think about many solutions to a problem at once, and it's a form of cognitive flexibility that can lead to high creativity. Many individuals with ADHD can connect seemingly unrelated ideas, think outside the box, and come up with original solutions that might not occur to others. This ability can be a tremendous asset in fields that value innovation and creativity, from artistic endeavors to problem-solving in technology and engineering.

Given the mixed bag that is cognitive flexibility in ADHD, developing strategies to enhance this ability can provide significant benefits. One effective method is engaging in activities that challenge the brain in new and diverse ways. This could be anything from learning a new language to playing strategy-based games like chess or engaging in creative activities like painting or writing. These activities encourage the brain to form new connections and can improve mental agility over time. Another helpful approach is to practice switching tasks intentionally in a controlled way. For example, you might set a timer and switch between different activities at set intervals, gradually decreasing the time spent on each task. This method can help train your brain to switch gears more smoothly and reduce the stress and resistance often experienced during transitions.

Adopting a more flexible daily schedule can also be incredibly beneficial. This might seem counterintuitive, especially since structured routines are often recommended for managing ADHD. However, incorporating planned flexibility into your day can allow you to take advantage of your natural workflow and energy fluctuations throughout the day. For instance, you might block out periods for deep-focused work but leave the specific tasks to be decided immediately based on your current mental state and priorities. This strategy combines structure with the flexibility to adapt to the brain's natural inclinations, reducing frustration and increasing productivity.

Embracing cognitive flexibility as a concept and actively working to improve it offers a powerful way to not just cope with ADHD, but to thrive. By recognizing and nurturing the natural creativity that often accompanies ADHD and developing strategies to enhance mental agility, you can transform potential obstacles into opportunities for growth and innovation. Whether through brain-training exercises, creative pursuits, or flexible scheduling, improving your cognitive flexibility can lead to significant improvements in both personal and professional realms. As you continue to explore and apply these strategies, you'll likely find that what once seemed like insurmountable challenges can become manageable—and even enjoyable—parts of your life.

Impulse Control: Why It's Hard and How to Improve

At its core, **impulse control** is about the ability to pause, think, and then act. It's an essential part of regulating our behaviors and responses to situations. When functioning optimally, impulse control helps us resist the urge to say something hurtful in anger, decide against buying a luxury item we can't afford, or choose to start a project earlier rather than leave it to the last minute. This ability acts like a brake system in a car, helping us slow down and make better decisions rather than speeding towards potential mistakes.

However, for those of us navigating the world with ADHD, this 'brake system' can often be less reliable. Impulse control is intricately linked with executive functioning, where the ADHD brain exhibits noticeable challenges. The result? A propensity towards hasty decisions or actions without fully considering the consequences. This might manifest as interrupting others during conversations, making spontaneous purchases, or jumping from one task to another without completing any of them. These aren't choices made from a lack of awareness or care; instead, they're often the byproducts of how an ADHD brain is wired. Neurobiologically, ADHD is associated with decreased activity in the frontal lobe—particularly areas responsible for executive function, including impulse control. This can shorten the pause between thought and action, leading to more impulsive, less deliberate behaviors.

The ripple effects of these impulse control challenges can touch all corners of life. Consider financial impulsivity, which can lead to significant stress. Without the guardrails of effective impulse control, one might find themselves making frequent, unnecessary purchases, each seeming justified at the moment, only to face the stress of financial overextension later. In relationships, poor impulse control can result in saying things without thinking, hurting loved ones, and leading to misunderstandings or conflicts. Professionally, it might look like accepting too many projects without considering current workload capacities, thus affecting work performance and reliability.

Addressing these challenges requires practical strategies tailored to strengthen impulse control. One effective approach is **delaying gratification,** a technique that can be honed through small, daily exercises. For instance, you may wait an hour before responding to an email that has triggered an immediate, emotional reaction. This brief period allows the initial impulse to pass, providing space for a more considered response. Another technique involves setting up reward systems that encourage more extended periods of focus or task completion before engaging in more pleasurable activities. This could look like working for an hour on a report before taking a break to check social media, gradually increasing the work period over time to build endurance for sustained attention.

Cognitive restructuring, a method used in cognitive-behavioral therapy, also offers a powerful way to improve impulse control. This technique involves identifying and challenging the automatic thoughts that often lead to impulsive actions. For example, if you find yourself thinking, "I need to buy this now," cognitive restructuring would encourage you to examine this thought for accuracy and helpfulness, potentially reshaping it to, "I want this now, but I can wait and decide if it's necessary after I consider my budget." This reevaluation process can diminish the urgency of the impulse, allowing for more deliberate decision-making.

Integrating these strategies into daily routines can become part of a new way of navigating impulses. This doesn't just help avoid the downsides of impulsive decisions but also enhances overall well-being by fostering a sense of control and reducing the chaos that impulsivity can bring. Whether it's through delaying gratification, setting up rewards, or reshaping thoughts, improving impulse control is a critical step towards a more balanced and manageable life with ADHD. With each small victory, the seemingly relentless tide of impulsivity can be turned into a more navigable current, guiding you towards better choices and a more fulfilling life.

***

Terms

- **Attention Deficit Hyperactivity Disorder (ADHD):** a neurodevelopmental disorder, one that significantly impacts the executive functions of the brain, which govern our ability to plan, organize, and regulate our behavior

- **Prefrontal cortex:** located at the front of the brain, the part of the brain that is responsible for high-level decision-making and problem-solving

- **Dopamine:** a neurotransmitter, often called the "feel-good" hormone, but it's also deeply involved in attention and motivation

- **Time blindness**: the difficulty in understanding and managing the passage of time

- **Emotional dysregulation:** difficulties in controlling emotional responses to various situations

- **Cognitive-behavioral strategies:** recognizing the thoughts that trigger emotional responses and learning to reframe them in ways that lead to more balanced emotions

- **Cognitive flexibility:** the ability to swiftly and effectively shift your thoughts and adapt your behaviors in response to new information, changing conditions, or unexpected obstacles

- **Impulse control:** the ability to pause, think, and then act

- **Delaying gratification:** a technique that can be honed through small, daily exercises in order to gain impulse control

- **Cognitive restructuring:** a technique that involves identifying and challenging the automatic thoughts that often lead to impulsive actions

STRATEGY #1
STRATEGIC TIME MANAGEMENT

You're standing at the entrance of a bustling amusement park, filled with exciting rides and attractions. The possibilities are endless, and each ride looks more thrilling than the last. Deciding where to go first can be overwhelming. Now, consider that this amusement park is your daily task list. For those of us with ADHD, determining which task to tackle first can often feel just as bewildering. This is where strategic time management comes into play, acting as that friend who knows the park inside out, suggesting which ride to go on first based on what you enjoy, what's less crowded, or what will give you the best overall experience.

Prioritizing with ADHD: Techniques That Really Work

Identifying Priority Tasks

One of the most effective ways to manage your day-to-day tasks is learning how to prioritize them. I know what you're thinking: "Easier said than done." And you're right, especially when every task seems to shout "urgent"! This is where the **Eisenhower Box**, a simple yet powerful tool, can help.

	URGENT	NOT URGENT
IMPORTANT	**DO:** Do it now.	**DECIDE:** Schedule a time to do it.
NOT IMPORTANT	**DELEGATE:** Who can do it for you?	**DELETE:** Eliminate it.

The Eisenhower Box

The top two categories are Urgent and Not Urgent, and the side two are Important and Not Important. This matrix allows you to categorize tasks in a way that visually breaks down what needs your immediate attention

(Urgent and Important), what should be scheduled (Important but Not Urgent), what can be delegated (Urgent but Not Important), and what you might want to drop (Neither Urgent nor Important). For someone with ADHD, this visual method of prioritizing tasks can be a game-changer. It helps move decision-making from a chaotic mental exercise to a clear, structured format.

Using Visual Tools for Clarity

Speaking of visual aids, tools like Kanban boards and priority matrices are not just trendy office accessories. They are particularly beneficial for ADHD minds. A Kanban board, for example, can be a physical board or a digital app where tasks are moved from one column to another—typically from To Do, to Doing, to Done. This method offers a clear visual representation of your workload and provides the satisfaction of moving tasks to the completed section, which can be incredibly motivating. Similarly, priority matrices can be used to visually categorize tasks based on urgency and importance, reducing the mental clutter that often accompanies decision-making about what to tackle next.

TO DO	IN PROGRESS	REVIEW	DONE
Task 1	Task 4	Task 3	Task 6
Task 2		Task 5	

Kanban Board

The Role of Decision-Making in Prioritization

Now, let's talk about the decision-making process itself. Prioritizing tasks effectively often requires quick and decisive thinking—a common challenge for those with ADHD. The trick here is to simplify the decision-making process. Once you've used tools like the Eisenhower Box or a Kanban board, permit yourself to choose three tasks that seem most critical and focus solely on these for the day. This limit helps prevent you from believing you must do everything at once. It's about giving yourself the space to focus intensely on a few tasks rather than spreading your attention too thinly across many.

Customization of Prioritization Techniques

Finally, the beauty of these tools and techniques lies in their flexibility. **Customization is key**. What works for one person might not work for another, and that's perfectly okay. If the classic Kanban board layout doesn't suit you, tweak it. Maybe you need a column for "Waiting on Someone Else" or "Ideas to Explore Later." Adjust these tools to fit your workflow and personal style better. The goal is to make these strategies work for you, not to mold yourself to them. By personalizing these methods, you adhere more naturally to them, and they become more than just strategies—they become your strategies, tailored tools that enhance your unique way of managing time and tasks.

In the grand buffet of tasks and responsibilities that each day presents, having a clear, customized way to prioritize what's on your plate can transform feelings of overwhelm into feelings of accomplishment. Whether using a visual aid like the Eisenhower Box to categorize tasks or personalizing a Kanban board to track your progress, the right tools can help you navigate your day with greater confidence and efficiency. Remember, the goal isn't to get everything done; instead, it's to focus on getting the right things done, reducing stress, and enhancing your productivity in a way that feels manageable and enjoyable.

Overcoming Procrastination: Steps to Start and Sustain Tasks

Procrastination isn't just about laziness or poor time management; for many of us with ADHD, it's a complex behavioral pattern rooted in emotional responses such as fear of failure or being overwhelmed by the size and scope of tasks. Understanding these roots can provide significant insights into why starting a task feels daunting. Let's peel back the layers a bit. Imagine you have a big project due—a presentation, perhaps. The fear of not performing well or the anxiety of facing an enormous, complex task can trigger a freeze response. To protect you from these uncomfortable feelings, your brain convinces you to avoid the task. Suddenly, cleaning your entire house seems like a more reasonable thing to do than outlining a few slides. This is procrastination in action: a defense mechanism against stress and anxiety, not a personal flaw.

Breaking tasks into manageable pieces is a practical method to counteract this. It's about changing how you view the task from a monolithic chore to a series of small, achievable steps. Let's stick with the presentation example. Instead of looking at it as one huge task, break it down: today, you could draft just the introduction; tomorrow, outline one section, and so on. Each piece feels less intimidating, and starting becomes less of a hurdle. This method reduces the mental and emotional weight of the task, making the activation energy needed to begin much lower. It's like turning a mountain into a series of small hills.

Incorporating motivational techniques can also play a crucial role in managing procrastination. One such technique is the "**five-minute start.**" Commit to working on a task for just five minutes. Tell yourself you can stop after five minutes if it feels too much. What this does is it lowers the stakes of engagement. Often, starting feels like the most challenging part, but by reducing the task to just five minutes, you trick your brain into making the first move; sometimes, all you need is to break the inertia. More often than not, once you start, you'll find it easier to keep going beyond the initial commitment. The five-minute start is a gentle nudge that can lead to sustained engagement.

Sustaining task engagement once you've started is another challenge. ADHD can make it difficult to maintain focus and motivation, especially if a task is lengthy or complex. Setting **mini-deadlines** and using rewards can effectively keep your momentum going. Mini-deadlines work by creating a series of finish lines throughout the task. For instance, you might set a goal to finish the introduction of your presentation by lunchtime. This creates a sense of urgency and progress, making the task feel more dynamic and less like a never-ending marathon. Pairing these mini-deadlines with small rewards can further enhance motivation. Have you finished the introduction on time? Reward yourself with a 10-minute break, a small treat, or whatever feels like a positive reinforcement for your effort.

These strategies aren't just about getting things done. They're about changing your relationship with work and tasks. They transform your approach from avoidance and dread to a more engaging and manageable experience. By understanding the emotional roots of procrastination, breaking tasks into smaller segments, tricking your brain into getting started, and keeping the momentum with mini-deadlines and rewards, you can turn the anxiety-inducing act of beginning into a series of successful completions. This boosts your productivity and builds a positive feedback loop, where each small success fuels the next, gradually chipping away at the habit of procrastination. Embracing these strategies can significantly affect how you manage tasks and how you feel about your ability to tackle them, leading to a more productive and less stressful work process.

The Power of Time Blocking for Unpredictable ADHD Minds

Time blocking might sound like a buzzword from a trendy productivity seminar, but it's a profoundly effective tool, especially for those of us navigating the whirlwind of ADHD. Time blocking involves dividing your day into chunks of time, each dedicated to a specific task or type of task. This method is more than just scheduling; it's about creating a visual map of your day that delineates when you'll focus on different activities. For someone with ADHD, whose time perception might often feel like a tangled ball of yarn, this approach helps by providing structure and clarity. It's like having railings on a winding staircase; they guide you and prevent you from straying off the path.

Setting up a time-blocking system can be a game-changer, and it's more manageable than it might seem. Start by evaluating your typical day or week: What tasks must you accomplish? Which are high priority? How much time do you realistically need for each? Begin by blocking out the non-negotiables—such as work hours, appointments, or time for meals and rest. Next, look at the tasks you need to accomplish. Assign fixed blocks of time to these tasks, and here's the ADHD-specific twist: keep these blocks shorter than you think you might need. Why? Because our perception of time tends to expand tasks to fill available space. Limiting time blocks to, say, 30 minutes instead of an hour creates a sense of urgency that can help maintain focus.

Flexibility within this structure is crucial. Our brains thrive on novelty, and a schedule that is too rigid can feel suffocating and counterproductive. To incorporate flexibility, intersperse your task blocks with open blocks—short periods where nothing is scheduled. These can be used for overflows, where a task might need more time than anticipated, or for breaks, which are vital for preventing cognitive overload and keeping your brain fresh. Additionally, having a couple of flexible blocks in your day can accommodate the spontaneous nature of ADHD, allowing for those bursts of creativity or unexpected events without throwing off your entire schedule.

Time	Activity	Time	Activity
7:00 AM	BREAKFAST	2:00 PM	SOLO WORK
7:30 AM	CALENDAR PLANNING/EMAILS	2:30 PM	BREAK
8:00 AM	MEETING 1	3:00 PM	MEETING 5
8:30 AM	NOTES ON MEETING / ACTION STEPS	3:30 PM	NOTES ON MEETING/ ACTION STEPS
9:00 AM	MEETING 2	4:00 PM	BREAK/SNACK
9:30 AM	BREAK/SNACK	4:30 PM	REVIEW ACTION STEPS/ PLAN WEEK
10:00 AM	NOTES ON MEETING/ ACTION STEPS	5:00 PM	REST
10:30 AM	MEETING 3	5:30 PM	WORKOUT
11:00 AM	NOTES ON MEETING/ ACTION STEPS	6:00 PM	WORKOUT
11:30 AM	SOLO WORK/EMAILS	6:30 PM	DINNER
12:00 PM	LUNCH	7:00 PM	REST
12:30 PM	PREP FOR AFTERNOON TASKS	7:30 PM	READING
1:00 PM	MEETING 4	8:00 PM	PREP FOR TOMORROW
1:30 PM	NOTES ON MEETING/ ACTION STEPS	8:30 PM	GET READY FOR BED

Sample: Time Blocking

Let's bring this concept to life with some success stories. Consider Jamie, a freelance graphic designer with ADHD, who found herself constantly overwhelmed by fluctuating deadlines and her creative process, which she felt she couldn't control. By implementing time blocking, Jamie could designate blocks for client work, creative brainstorming, and administrative tasks. She kept her mornings free for creative work when her energy was highest, followed by client interactions in the afternoon, using her flexible blocks to adjust as needed based on the day's demands. This improved her productivity and significantly reduced her stress levels, as she could see and manage her time more effectively.

Another case is Mark, a high school teacher struggling with lesson planning, grading, and his coursework for an advanced degree. Through time blocking, Mark dedicated early mornings to grading, reserved school hours for teaching and interacting with students, and set evening hours for his coursework, with strict blocks for family time during dinner. This structure helped him manage his responsibilities without feeling like he was constantly playing catch-up. What's more, the precise boundaries around family time helped improve his relationships, which his previously erratic schedule had strained.

Time blocking, specially tailored for the ADHD mind, provides more than just a schedule. It offers a framework that respects our unique perception of time and our need for structure balanced with flexibility. By defining what you're supposed to focus on and when and incorporating necessary breaks and flexible periods, this approach can transform how you manage your days. It turns the abstract concept of time into a tangible, manageable mosaic of tasks and breaks, which can lead to a more productive, less stressful life. Whether you're a student, a professional, or anything in between, understanding and implementing time blocking can equip you with the tools to navigate your day and conquer it.

> *What method are you most interested in?* The Eisenhower Box, Kanban Boards, or Time Blocking?

Setting Realistic Deadlines and Meeting Them

When it comes to managing tasks, setting deadlines is the equivalent of drawing finish lines; they mark the point you need to reach, guiding your pace and effort. However, for those of us with ADHD, these finish lines can sometimes seem to blur or move, making it hard to hit them accurately. We often struggle with time estimation, which is crucial for setting **realistic deadlines.** Have you ever started what you thought was a thirty-minute task only to find two hours later that you're only halfway through? This mismatch between expected and actual time needed is a common issue. It stems from our unique neurological wiring, which affects our ability to judge the duration of tasks accurately.

Improving this skill starts with awareness and practice. Begin by tracking how long it takes to complete daily tasks rather than how long you think they should take. You can use a simple timer or a time-tracking app specifically designed for this purpose. This isn't about critiquing your speed; it's about gathering data to understand your unique pace better. As you collect more information, you'll start to notice patterns and can adjust your future estimates accordingly. This method not only improves your ability to set more realistic deadlines but also reduces the stress and frustration from unexpected time crunches.

Adding buffer time to your deadlines is another strategy that can be particularly effective. Think of buffer time as building a little fence around your task's timeline—it's there to protect against unexpected interruptions or when you fall into a state of hyperfocus and lose track of time. A good rule of thumb is to add a 20% buffer to the time you think a task will take. If you estimate a project will take five hours, give yourself an additional hour. This extra time can absorb the impact of distractions or provide extra minutes if a task is more complex than initially thought. It's a way of planning for the unpredictable, which, let's face it, is often a part of our daily experience.

The concept of an accountability partner might sound formal, but it can be as casual as having a friend, family member, or colleague who understands your goals and can help you stay on track. This person is a gentle reminder of your commitments and can be a source of motivation and support. For instance, setting a weekly check-in to discuss progress on your tasks can create a consistent structure that helps maintain momentum. They don't need to be involved in the details of your projects; just knowing that someone will ask about your progress can increase your accountability and drive to meet deadlines.

Lastly, let's not forget the importance of celebrating milestones. Recognizing and celebrating progress is crucial for maintaining motivation, especially for long-term projects. When you meet a deadline, take a moment to celebrate that achievement in a way that feels rewarding. It could be as simple as taking a break to enjoy a favorite coffee or planning a small outing. These celebrations act as positive reinforcement, making you more likely to feel motivated to tackle the next deadline with the same energy. It's about creating a positive feedback loop where each success builds your confidence and propels you forward.

Setting realistic deadlines and meeting them consistently doesn't just help manage tasks more effectively; it also builds a sense of reliability and confidence in your abilities. By improving your time estimation skills, incorporating buffer times, utilizing the support of an accountability partner, and celebrating your milestones, you create a robust framework that supports not just completing tasks but also contributes to a more structured and successful management of your time and responsibilities. This approach allows you to navigate your commitments with clarity and reduces the chaos surrounding time management, especially for those of us with ADHD.

Tools and Apps to Enhance Time Awareness

In the digital age, where technology touches nearly every aspect of our lives, it's no surprise that numerous tools and apps are designed to assist with time management. For those of us with ADHD, these tools can be precious, acting as external extensions of our executive functions. They help bridge the gap between our intentions and actions, especially in managing time and tasks. Imagine having a personal assistant who constantly reminds you of what's next, helps you visualize your day, and keeps you from losing track of your goals. That's what these digital tools can do.

Let's explore some of the digital tools and apps that are particularly useful for us with ADHD. Apps like **Trello, Asana, and Todoist** allow you to create tasks, assign them to specific projects, and set deadlines. They also enable you to visualize tasks in various formats, whether a simple list, a calendar, or a Kanban board. What makes these tools so compelling is their ability to keep us organized and their adaptability. Each app can be customized to fit different needs and preferences. For instance, you can set up custom reminders in Todoist to alert you at specific times of the day or when you're at particular locations, ensuring that you're reminded of the right task at the right time and place. Similarly, Trello allows you to color-code tasks, making it easy to quickly identify what type of activity each task represents, whether it's a work-related project, a personal errand, or something else.

Customization is crucial because it turns a generic tool into a personal aide tailored to the unique ways your ADHD brain works. For example, suppose you know that you're likely to overlook a task unless it's visually prominent. In that case, you can customize these apps to highlight your most urgent tasks in red or to have them automatically move to the top of your list. You can also set up recurring reminders for tasks that need to be done regularly, which can help form habits and routines. This level of customization ensures that the tool adapts to your needs rather than forcing you to adapt, which can make all the difference in its effectiveness.

Integrating these tools into your daily life so they become a seamless part of your routine is another key to success. Start by choosing one or two tools that best meet your needs and spend some time setting them up in a way that feels intuitive and helpful. Use them consistently for a few weeks to manage your tasks and time. Set a reminder to check your chosen app each morning and throughout the day to reinforce the habit of using it. Over time, these tools can become natural extensions of your day, almost like a reflex. For instance, every morning, you might automatically open your Trello board to see the tasks lined up for the day, or you might enter any new task into Todoist right when it comes to mind, ensuring that it doesn't get forgotten.

While these tools are beneficial, it's essential to be aware of their limitations and potential pitfalls. One such limitation is the risk of becoming too reliant on these digital tools, so you might feel paralyzed without them. It's beneficial to occasionally practice managing your time and tasks without digital tools to maintain your innate skills in these areas. Another potential pitfall is the distraction that can come with technology. With smartphones and computers, the temptation to drift away from your task list and into social media or other online distractions is always a click away. To mitigate this, use features like app blockers or screen time limits to keep your focus on the task at hand.

Choosing the right tools, customizing them to fit your unique needs, and integrating them into your daily routine can significantly improve your ability to manage time and tasks. These digital aids can provide the external structure needed to navigate the challenges of ADHD, helping you to stay organized, focused, and productive. As you continue to use these tools, you'll likely find that managing your time becomes less about struggling with memory or motivation and more about making strategic choices that align with your goals and lifestyle, ultimately leading to a more structured and fulfilling day.

Creating Routines That Stick in the ADHD Brain

For us with ADHD, the word "routine" might conjure images of a monotonous, colorless life dictated by the repetitive ticking of a clock. However, establishing routines goes far beyond imposing a rigid schedule upon ourselves; it's about creating a framework that enhances our ability to navigate daily life more easily and with less stress. Think of a routine as a personalized roadmap that guides you through your day, reducing the mental load of constantly deciding what to do next. This is particularly beneficial for those of us with ADHD, as it alleviates the paralysis often caused by overwhelming choices and helps in managing time more effectively.

Building these routines, especially ones that stick, involves more than deciding what you want to do and when. It's about understanding your rhythms and creating a structure aligning with your best operations. Start by observing your natural tendencies. Are you a night owl who finds a burst of energy as the sun goes down, or are you up with the dawn, ready to tackle the world? Use these insights to schedule demanding tasks when you're most alert and creative tasks when you need less structure. The next step is to integrate these activities into your daily life gradually. Begin with one or two essential habits you want to develop, such as preparing for the next day each evening or setting aside time for emails in the morning. Anchor these new habits to existing ones to increase their stickiness. For instance, if you already have coffee every morning, use that time to review your daily tasks. This method of stacking habits can significantly enhance the likelihood of them becoming a seamless part of your routine.

The role of external cues in reinforcing these routines cannot be overstated. Our environment constantly influences our behavior, often without us even realizing it. By strategically placing visual reminders around your living or workspace, you can create cues that prompt you to stick to your routine. This could be as simple as putting your gym clothes next to your bed to encourage morning workouts or setting up a dedicated workspace for study equipped with all the necessary tools. Digital reminders can also be effective, especially if you forget tasks or lose track of time. Setting alarms on your phone or using apps that remind you to move on to the next task can help keep you on track throughout the day.

Flexibility is critical in maintaining routines, particularly for the ADHD brain, which craves novelty and can rebel against too much structure. It's important to allow your routines to evolve as your life changes. This could mean adjusting your schedule to accommodate a new job, changing family dynamics, or even shifting your interests and priorities. Regularly review and adjust your routines to ensure they continue to serve you well. This might involve setting aside time each week to reflect on what's working and what isn't and to make necessary adjustments. This process of continual refinement helps ensure that your routines remain effective and aligned with your current needs and goals.

In crafting routines that stick, you're essentially programming your environment to work for you. You reduce the mental clutter and make room for what truly matters. Whether it's making sure you have time for your passions, meeting your professional obligations, or simply carving out moments for relaxation, a well-crafted routine can transform how you experience and manage your day. As you move through this process, remember that the goal is not to fill every minute with activity but to create a framework that gives you the freedom to live more fully, with ADHD not as a barrier but as a part of who you are.

In wrapping up this chapter on Strategic Time Management, we've explored various strategies to help you manage your time more effectively, from understanding and using tools like the Eisenhower Box for breaking tasks into manageable pieces and establishing routines that align with your unique needs. Each strategy offers a way to harness the often chaotic energy of ADHD, channeling it into productive and fulfilling activities. As we transition into the next chapter, we'll build on these foundations, delving into enhancing focus and productivity, where you'll learn to fine-tune these strategies and apply them in ways that significantly boost your efficiency and reduce your stress. Remember, the journey to mastering time management with ADHD is ongoing, and each step you take builds on the last, moving you closer to a more organized, purposeful life.

***

Tools & Techniques

- **Eisenhower Box:** This matrix allows you to categorize tasks in a way that visually breaks down what needs your immediate attention (Urgent and Important), what should be scheduled (Important but Not Urgent), what can be delegated (Urgent but Not Important), and what you might want to drop (Neither Urgent nor Important)

- **Kanban Board:** a physical board or a digital app where tasks are moved from one column to another—typically from To Do, to Doing, to Done

- **Five-Minute Start:** working on a task for just five minutes

- **Time Blocking:** a framework that respects our unique perception of time and our need for structure balanced with flexibility. A schedule to focus incorporating necessary breaks and flexible periods,

- **Accountability Partner:** a friend, family member, or colleague who understands your goals and can help you stay on track

STRATEGY #2
ENHANCING FOCUS AND PRODUCTIVITY

Picture this: you're in a cozy cafe, surrounded by the gentle murmur of conversation and the soft aroma of coffee. It's the perfect setting to get some work done. Yet, two hours later, you find you've barely scratched the surface of your tasks. Sounds familiar? For many of us living with ADHD, maintaining focus isn't just about finding the right environment; it's a daily challenge, a puzzle we perpetually solve. This chapter is your toolbox, filled with strategies and insights designed to enhance your focus and boost productivity in ways that align with the unique workings of your ADHD mind.

The Focus Formula: Techniques for Sustained Attention

Understanding Focus in ADHD

The concept of sustained attention, or the ability to maintain focus on a task over time, can sometimes feel like a foreign language in ADHD. It's not that we don't want to focus; instead, our brains are wired to seek novelty and change, making sustained attention particularly challenging. This can often result in a frustrating cycle of starting tasks with good intentions, only to find our minds wandering to a dozen other thoughts within minutes. Addressing this requires a personalized strategy that understands the nuances of your focus patterns rather than trying to fit into a one-size-fits-all solution.

Single-Tasking vs. Multi-Tasking

In a world that often glorifies the art of multi-tasking, it might come as a surprise that single-tasking is more effective, especially for ADHD brains. While multitasking might make you feel productive, studies have shown that our brains aren't truly focusing on multiple things at once; instead, we are just switching rapidly between tasks, which can be exhausting and inefficient. For those of us with ADHD, this can lead to increased feelings of being overwhelmed and can diminish productivity. Embracing single-tasking involves focusing on one task at a time, which can significantly reduce the cognitive load, making it easier to maintain focus. Start by creating a distraction-free environment for your most important task of the day. This might mean turning off notifications on your phone or using apps that block distracting websites. *Allow yourself to immerse fully in the task at hand, giving it your undivided attention until a set break time.*

Focus-Enhancing Exercises

Incorporating specific exercises into your daily routine can be beneficial to train your brain to focus better. Attention training techniques, such as mindfulness meditation, have been shown to improve concentration and cognitive flexibility, which are crucial for enhancing focus in ADHD.

Mindfulness involves paying deliberate attention to the present moment in a non-judgmental way, which can help reduce the mind's tendency to wander. *Start with short, five-minute sessions daily, gradually increasing the duration as your attention span improves.* Another effective exercise is the practice of focused breathing, where you concentrate solely on your breath, bringing your focus back whenever your mind starts to drift. These exercises improve focus, reduce anxiety, and increase overall mental resilience.

Role of Medication and Natural Supplements

While lifestyle changes and exercises are crucial, they may need to be supplemented with medication or natural treatments. Many individuals with ADHD find that certain medications can significantly improve their ability to focus. These medications typically work by increasing levels of dopamine and norepinephrine in the brain, which help enhance attention and impulse control. *However, medication is not a one-size-fits-all solution and must be carefully managed under the guidance of a healthcare provider.* In addition to medication, some natural supplements, such as omega-3 fatty acids, zinc, and magnesium, have been found to support cognitive function in ADHD. Before starting any new medication or supplement, it's essential to consult with a healthcare provider to discuss the best options based on your specific needs and medical history.

In the tapestry of strategies to enhance focus, understanding the unique challenges of ADHD is just the starting thread. By embracing single-tasking, engaging in focus-enhancing exercises, and considering the role of medication and supplements, you can tailor a focus strategy that fits your life. This is not about fixing something broken; it's about understanding and optimizing how your brain works, turning potential obstacles into stepping stones toward greater productivity and fulfillment.

> **Mindful Take-away:**
>
> First step to discovering your ideal strategy for focus and productivity is knowing that nothing is one-size-fits-all. One solution that works for one person may not work for another. Maybe it might be a combination of solutions that will work for you. Overall, take your time to find what works best for you.

Managing Distractions in a Hyper-Connected World

Let's be honest, the digital age, for all its conveniences, sometimes feels tailor-made to disrupt a focus-challenged mind like ours. Every beep, buzz, and blink from our devices can pull us away from tasks that require deep focus. Recognizing what specifically draws our attention away is the first step in reclaiming our productivity. For many of us, the smartphone acts as the main culprit, with its constant notifications and the lure of social media just a tap away. Understanding these triggers, whether it's the ping of a new email or the pop-up of a news alert, can help us start to control them rather than letting them control our day.

Reducing digital distractions is crucial, and there are several practical steps you can take right now. Begin by auditing the notifications on your phone and computer. Ask yourself which ones are truly necessary. Does your email need to interrupt you with each new message? Most likely, no. Adjust your settings to allow only critical notifications. For those of us with ADHD, this small step can significantly reduce the digital noise that disrupts our workflow. Apps that block distracting websites during work hours can also be a game-changer. Tools like Freedom or Cold Turkey allow you to temporarily block your access to websites that might pull your focus away, like social media or news sites, helping you stay on track with your current task.

Creating a physical workspace that minimizes distractions is another transformative strategy. This goes beyond just having a tidy desk. It involves setting up an environment that actively encourages focus. For instance, consider the ergonomics of your workspace. A comfortable chair, a desk at the right height, and adequate lighting can reduce physical discomfort, which can often be a distraction.

Furthermore, **personalize your space** with items that reduce stress without causing distractions. This could be a plant, a piece of art, or a photo of a loved one—anything that brings a sense of calm. Ensure the essentials are within easy reach to minimize the need to get up frequently, which can open the door to other distractions.

Now, let's talk about regaining focus once it's lost—a common challenge for those with ADHD. **Cognitive restructuring techniques** can be incredibly effective here. This involves changing the way you think about focus and distractions. For instance, if you think, "I can never stay focused," reframe this thought to be more forgiving and constructive, such as "Everyone gets distracted sometimes, but I can improve my focus with practice." This kind of positive self-talk can reduce the frustration that often accompanies focus struggles, making it easier to gently guide your attention back to the task.

In this hyper-connected era, managing distractions is more than just willpower; it's about setting yourself up for success through **environment control, technology management, and cognitive awareness**. By identifying your personal distraction triggers and employing strategic measures to mitigate them, you create a conducive space for sustained concentration. This isn't about eliminating all distractions—that's an unrealistic goal. Rather, it's about understanding and managing these interruptions so they don't derail your productivity and mental well-being. Through these strategies, you can transform your work environment from a battlefield of distractions into a fortress of focus, where you can harness your energies to achieve more with a sense of control and accomplishment.

The Role of Physical Environment in ADHD Productivity

Imagine stepping into a workspace that feels like a breath of fresh air—where each element, from the lighting to your desk arrangement, is tailored to enhance focus and productivity. For those of us with ADHD, the physical environment can play a pivotal role in how well we concentrate and maintain productivity throughout the day. It's not just about aesthetics; it's about creating an environment that actively supports our unique needs.

The optimal environment for focus for someone with ADHD often involves a careful balance of sensory inputs. **Lighting,** for example, can have a significant impact. Natural light is ideal as it not only brightens the space but also helps improve mood and energy levels, which are crucial for maintaining focus. If natural light isn't an option, choosing full-spectrum light bulbs can mimic the feel of natural light, providing a similar boost. Noise levels are another critical factor. While some of us need complete quiet to focus, others may find gentle background noise, like white noise or soft music, helpful in masking more disruptive sounds. The key is understanding what works best for you and trying to create that balance in your workspace.

Now, let's dive deeper into setting up a workspace that supports productivity. **Ergonomics** plays a crucial role here. An uncomfortable chair or a desk that's too high or too low can be distracting and even lead to physical discomfort, pulling your focus away from tasks. Investing in an ergonomic chair that supports your spine and allows your feet to rest flat on the floor can make a significant difference. Similarly, positioning your computer screen at eye level helps avoid neck strain. Organizational tools are equally important. Consider using desk organizers or drawer dividers to keep your workspace tidy. A cluttered desk can lead to a cluttered mind, which is the last thing you need when trying to focus. Labeling drawers and using color-coded folders for different projects can also help reduce the time spent searching for items, streamline your workflow, and keep you in the zone.

Incorporating **elements of nature** into your workspace can also enhance cognitive function and focus. Studies have shown that being around nature or viewing scenes of nature can reduce stress, enhance creativity, and improve focus. If you can, position your desk near a window with a view of trees or the sky. Alternatively, adding some indoor plants to your workspace can bring a slice of nature indoors. Not only do plants enhance the aesthetic quality of your space, but they also improve air quality, which can boost brain function and overall well-being.

Regular changes in your physical workspace can also prevent habituation, a common issue where the novelty of a new setup wears off, reducing its effectiveness in maintaining your focus. This could be as simple as rearranging your desk, changing the artwork on the walls, or even altering your digital desktop's layout. These changes can help keep your environment stimulating, which is particularly important in maintaining attention for those with ADHD. It's like giving your brain a little jolt, reminding it to stay engaged and attentive.

Creating a focus-friendly workspace isn't just about making things look nice; it's about crafting an environment that actively supports your efforts to manage ADHD. By considering factors like lighting, noise levels, ergonomics, and the presence of nature, you can create a space that looks welcoming and enhances your ability to concentrate and be productive. Remember, the goal is to build an environment that feels like it's working with you, not against you, turning your workspace into a powerful ally in your quest for enhanced focus and productivity.

Task Initiation and Follow-Through: Building Momentum

Initiating a task can sometimes feel like starting a car on a freezing morning; it takes a few tries, a little patience, and sometimes, a lot of frustration. For those of us with ADHD, this scenario can be a frequent reality, known as initiation paralysis. It's that daunting feeling of standing at the base of a mountain, knowing you need to start climbing but unable to make the first step. Overcoming this begins with understanding that it's not about a lack of desire to accomplish tasks but how ADHD affects the brain's executive functions, making starting tasks particularly challenging.

One effective strategy to combat initiation paralysis is the use of **starting rituals**. These personalized routines signal to your brain that it's time to transition into work mode. For instance, you might start your workday by making a cup of tea, arranging your workspace, and then spending a few minutes reviewing your to-do list. This ritual acts like a warm-up for your brain, easing the transition into task mode. Another powerful technique is the "two-minute rule." If a task can be done in two minutes or less, do it immediately. This rule helps by breaking down the psychological barrier of starting, often the most challenging part of a task. Once you're in motion, it's easier to keep moving forward, turning the dread of initiation into the satisfaction of action.

Maintaining **momentum** once a task has begun is equally crucial. Momentum, like a boulder rolling down a hill, builds on itself. However, keeping it going requires conscious effort, especially in an ADHD mind prone to distractions and shifts in focus. **Progress tracking is an invaluable tool here.** By setting clear, measurable milestones within a task, you provide yourself with a roadmap and visible markers of your progress. These markers are continual motivation; each small achievement fuels your drive to reach the next.

Additionally, strategic use of breaks can significantly enhance your productivity. **The Pomodoro Technique**, involving intervals of focused work followed by short breaks, can be particularly effective. It aligns well with the ADHD need for frequent shifts in focus, preventing burnout and keeping your mind fresh and engaged. *(Refer to the Pomodoro Technique later in the chapter.)*

Accountability systems form another cornerstone of successful task completion. These systems can be digital, like a project management tool that sends reminders about deadlines, or interpersonal, such as regular check-ins with a coworker or coach. The key is consistency and a degree of external oversight, which can significantly enhance your commitment to a task. For example, if you know that you'll be discussing your progress on a project in a weekly meeting, you're more likely to dedicate focused effort toward advancing in that project. This external motivation can be particularly effective in overcoming the ADHD tendency to procrastinate or switch tasks prematurely.

Celebrating small wins is one of the most overlooked yet essential strategies for maintaining long-term productivity. Each task completed, each small goal met, is a victory that deserves recognition. This isn't about grand gestures but acknowledging your efforts and successes along the way. This could be as simple as reflecting on what you've accomplished at the end of the day or treating yourself to a coffee after finishing a challenging task. These celebrations enhance your motivation and help build a positive association with task completion, reinforcing your desire to follow through in the future.

Integrating these strategies into your daily routine transforms the challenge of task initiation and follow-through from a daunting ordeal into a series of manageable, even enjoyable steps. Each strategy builds upon the other, creating a robust framework that supports sustained productivity and a more rewarding approach to managing tasks. By adapting these methods to fit your unique needs and lifestyle, you empower yourself to start tasks with confidence and see them through to completion, creating a cycle of productivity and success that fuels your personal and professional growth.

Mind Mapping for ADHD: Organizing Thoughts Visually

Imagine if there was a way to visually plot out your thoughts, ideas, and tasks in a way that not only organizes them but also makes them easier to process and remember. Well, there is, and it's called **mind mapping.** This technique is particularly effective for those of us with ADHD, as it taps into our inherent preference for visual learning and thinking. Mind mapping is a dynamic way to capture your thoughts and ideas around a central theme, spreading like branches on a tree. Each branch represents a different aspect or sub-topic of the main idea, making complex information structured yet easily digestible. For the ADHD brain, which often juggles scattered thoughts and struggles with linear planning, this method can be a breakthrough, simplifying thought processes and enhancing memory retention by linking concepts visually.

When you create a mind map, you start with a central concept placed in the middle of a blank page, and from this central idea, you draw branches that represent related topics or tasks. These can further divide into smaller branches, creating a sprawling visual representation of your thoughts. The beauty of this technique lies in its flexibility and creativity. You can use colors, symbols, and images to differentiate between themes, which not only makes the map more visually engaging but also aids in memory by creating distinct visual cues. The nonlinear nature of mind mapping allows for a natural flow of ideas, which can be remarkably liberating if you find traditional note-taking or list-making restrictive or uninspiring.

Mind Mapping

Choose tools that suit your style and needs to begin creating effective mind maps. You can start simply with a piece of paper and colored pens or use digital tools like XMind, MindMeister, or Microsoft Visio, which offer more features like templates and the ability to edit and share your maps easily. Start with a clear central idea and allow yourself to explore different branches as they come to you without worrying about order or structure. This can be particularly freeing, as it allows your ADHD brain to operate in its natural, exploratory mode. As your branches form, you can start to organize and prioritize them, using colors and symbols to categorize and make connections clearer. This process helps in organizing your thoughts and clarifying them, often leading to insights and solutions that might have yet to be apparent in a more linear format.

Mind mapping can be applied in various aspects of life and work. In your personal life, it can be used for **planning events, setting goals, or even as a journaling tool** to explore your thoughts and feelings. Professionally, mind maps can be invaluable for **project planning, brainstorming sessions, or breaking down complex tasks** into manageable steps. For example, if you're working on a project, you can create a mind map to outline different aspects, such as objectives, needed resources, potential challenges, and milestones. This visual overview helps keep your project organized and makes it easier to track progress and communicate with others.

Integrating mind maps with other productivity tools can further enhance your organizational strategies. For instance, you can **convert the tasks identified in your mind maps into a to-do list** in a task management app or use them as a reference in your digital calendar to schedule deadlines and reminders. This integration ensures that the visual planning and brainstorming facilitated by mind mapping translate into actionable steps, closing the loop from ideation to execution. By combining mind mapping with other tools, you create a comprehensive system that caters to the visual, creative strengths of your ADHD brain while also providing the structure and reminders needed to stay on track.

In employing mind mapping, you harness a powerful visual tool that aligns with the natural workings of your ADHD mind, fostering creativity, clarity, and organization. Whether you're planning your next big project, organizing your thoughts on a complex topic, or simply trying to capture fleeting ideas, mind mapping offers a flexible, effective way to bring structure to chaos, turning the swirling cloud of your thoughts into a clear, organized map that guides you towards your goals.

> **Tips for Mind Mapping:**
>
> ● **Start on paper to get used to the process** – this way you can see how far your map should go when you start from the center and move out
>
> ● **Feel free to use different colors** – you can label the colors for specific areas of work you want to focus on or for the urgency of tasks
>
> ● **Create a to-do list for the complex tasks** – transfer the tasks to a to-do list and then put them in a time-blocked calendar

Pomodoro and Beyond: Tailored Techniques for ADHD

The Pomodoro Technique, a time management method developed by Francesco Cirillo in the late 1980s, is based on breaking work into intervals—traditionally 25 minutes long—separated by short breaks. Each interval is known as a "Pomodoro," named after the tomato-shaped kitchen timer Cirillo used. This technique is particularly effective for individuals with ADHD for several reasons. First, it breaks down work into manageable chunks, reducing the overwhelm that can come with large tasks. Secondly, the scheduled breaks keep the mind fresh and attentive, which is crucial in managing the ADHD tendency towards mental fatigue and distraction.

However, the traditional Pomodoro intervals may not be a perfect fit for everyone, especially for those of us with ADHD, whose attention spans can vary significantly. **Customizing the length of work and break periods can make this technique much more effective.** For example, if your focus starts to wane after just 15 minutes, adjust the work intervals to be shorter. Alternatively, if you can dive deep into a task and maintain focus for longer than 25 minutes, extending the work intervals to 35 or 40 minutes might be beneficial. The key is to observe how long you can work effectively before you need a break and then tailor the Pomodoro settings to fit your rhythm.

Venturing beyond the Pomodoro Technique, other time management methods resonate better with different tasks or personal preferences. Another effective method is the **52-17 rule**, where you work for 52 minutes and break for 17 minutes. This technique, based on the theory that longer concentration intervals can be maintained if followed by substantial breaks, might be suitable for tasks requiring deeper concentration.

Combining various focus-enhancing techniques can create a personalized and flexible productivity system that caters to your needs. Start by identifying the types of tasks you need to accomplish and how different techniques best suit each. For instance, use the Pomodoro Technique for tasks that require frequent breaks to maintain focus, such as reading or writing. For functions that are highly engaging and where time tends to fly by, such as creative projects or brainstorming sessions, the 52-17 method might be more appropriate. By using mind mapping at the planning stage, you can visually lay out the tasks and decide which technique to apply to each, integrating them into a cohesive plan.

This tailored approach not only respects the unique flow of your ADHD mind but also empowers you to manage your time and energy more effectively. It acknowledges that productivity isn't about pushing yourself to the limits; it's about working smarter, understanding your neurological needs, and adapting management strategies accordingly. As you experiment with these techniques, remember that flexibility is vital. Allow yourself the space to adjust and adapt as you discover what works best for you, transforming the often daunting task of time management into a more enjoyable and rewarding experience.

We've explored several strategies to enhance focus and boost productivity, tailored specifically for the ADHD mind. From understanding the nuances of sustained attention and managing digital and environmental distractions to employing customized time management techniques like the Pomodoro, time boxing, or the 52-17 rule, each strategy has been designed to align with your unique needs and preferences. As we move forward, remember that the essence of productivity lies not in filling every minute with work but in making each minute count by working in ways that play to your strengths and respect your limits. Up next, we'll delve into emotional intelligence and resilience, crucial skills that will further equip you to navigate the complexities of life with ADHD, ensuring that your journey toward personal and professional fulfillment is successful and sustainable.

Terms & Techniques:

Single-Tasking: Focusing on one task vs. multi-tasking. Give undivided attention until a set break time Mind

Mapping: visual technique of capturing thoughts and ideas around a central theme then creating branches to sub-topics, then tasks at hand

The Pomodoro Technique: time management method where you break your work into 25-minute long intervals then short breaks in between

52-17 rule: Like the Pomodoro technique but customized to 52 minute long work interval separated by 17-minute break intervals

STRATEGY #3
EMOTIONAL INTELLIGENCE AND RESILIENCE

Imagine you're at a work trying to focus on a task or project, but instead, you find yourself swept up in a whirlwind of emotions sparked by an offhand comment from a friend. Suddenly, you're not just battling external chaos but internal chaos as well. This scenario might resonate deeply if you're navigating life with ADHD, where emotional responses can often feel as loud and demanding as the world around you. In this chapter, we dive into the art of understanding and managing these emotional currents to steady the boat and sail smoothly, even through stormy weather.

Understanding and Managing ADHD Emotional Responses

Recognizing Emotional Triggers

For many of us with ADHD, certain situations or comments can trigger disproportionately strong emotional responses. Recognizing these triggers is the first step toward managing them. These triggers often tie back to common ADHD symptoms, such as sensitivity to criticism or a heightened response to sensory stimuli. For instance, you might find that a casual remark about your punctuality can spiral into intense feelings of inadequacy or defensiveness. By mapping out situations that draw out these responses, you can anticipate and prepare for them. Keeping a simple journal where you note down instances that sparked a strong emotional reaction can be incredibly helpful. Over time, patterns will emerge, providing clear insights into which environments or interactions trigger your emotional responses and setting the stage for you to handle them more adeptly.

Emotional Response Patterns in ADHD

The emotional landscape for someone with ADHD can often feature rapid mood swings and an intense reaction to seemingly minor events. This heightened emotional reactivity is about feeling more intensely and the struggle to return to a baseline emotional state. These patterns can be illustrated through case studies, such as that of Alex, a graphic designer who found that feedback sessions with clients could swing her from feeling competent and excited to doubtful and anxious within minutes. Understanding that these patterns are a standard part of the ADHD experience can be comforting. It also highlights the importance of strategies addressing these swift and intense emotional shifts, providing a buffer and tools to navigate them.

Strategies for Immediate Emotional Management

When an intense emotional wave hits, having strategies to manage it can make all the difference. Simple, immediate techniques such as **focused breathing exercises** can be powerful. For instance, the **4-4-8 technique,** where you breathe in for 4 seconds, hold for 4 seconds, and exhale for 8 seconds, can significantly help calm the nervous system and regain emotional equilibrium. **Short meditative breaks**, even just five minutes to step back, close your eyes, and refocus your thoughts, can also be beneficial. **Physical activities,** particularly those that require engagement, like jogging or even a brisk walk around the block, can help dissipate the energy that comes with intense emotions, redirect it, and allow for a return to a more balanced state.

Long-Term Emotional Regulation Techniques

While immediate techniques are crucial, developing long-term strategies for emotional regulation is equally important. Techniques such as **Cognitive Behavioral Therapy (CBT),** which has been adapted specifically for managing ADHD, can offer significant benefits. CBT focuses on identifying and changing unhelpful thought patterns that can trigger or worsen emotional distress. For someone with ADHD, this might involve challenging the "all-or-nothing" thinking that can turn a small mistake into a catastrophe in your mind or learning to recognize and adjust the perfectionistic tendencies that can lead to immense frustration and self-critical thoughts. Engaging regularly with a therapist who understands the nuances of ADHD can provide not just tools but also an external perspective that helps in navigating emotional turbulence more effectively. This journey towards better emotional regulation is not about dampening your natural responses but rather about understanding and managing them to enhance your quality of life and interpersonal relationships.

Through the exploration of these strategies, the aim is to equip you with a toolkit that helps you manage the storms and navigate daily life with more ease and confidence. Emotional intelligence and resilience in the context of ADHD isn't just about coping; it's about thriving, recognizing your emotional patterns, and using them as guides rather than obstacles. As we continue to explore these themes, the focus will remain on practical, actionable strategies that you can integrate into your life, fostering a deeper understanding of yourself and enhancing your interactions with the world around you.

Techniques for Building Emotional Resilience

When you live with ADHD, emotional resilience can sometimes feel like a foreign landscape, lush and inviting yet mysteriously hard to navigate. Understanding **emotional resilience** in the context of ADHD is about recognizing your capacity to bounce back from difficulties and manage life's ups and downs effectively. It's crucial because the very nature of ADHD involves navigating a maze of emotional highs and lows, where resilience acts not just as a buffer but as a crucial navigation tool.

Building this kind of resilience involves more than just wishful thinking; it requires practical, actionable strategies that resonate with the unique challenges of ADHD. Consider the power of **journaling,** a simple yet profoundly effective tool for enhancing emotional resilience. When you journal, you do more than just scribble on a page; you dialogue with yourself, exploring and unpacking the layers of your emotions and experiences. This process helps vent out immediate frustrations and spot patterns in your emotional responses that you might have overlooked. Over time, this insight allows you to anticipate and prepare for situations that might throw you off balance, giving you a firmer standing in your emotional landscape.

Engaging in **hobbies** is another resilience-building activity that often goes underrated. Hobbies bring joy, and in the whirlwind of emotions ADHD can get, they act like anchors, providing moments of calm and focus in a sea of chaos. Whether painting, hiking, coding, or dancing, hobbies offer an outlet for expression and distraction, pulling you away from stressors and allowing your mind to reset and recover. They reinforce your sense of self and personal achievement, buffering against the negative impacts of stress and reducing the risk of burnout.

Structured social interactions also play a pivotal role in building emotional resilience. ADHD can sometimes make social interactions challenging, leading to feelings of isolation or misunderstanding. By creating structured settings to engage with others, whether through support groups, social clubs, or regular outings with friends, you provide yourself with a safety net of social support. These interactions offer perspective, understanding, and validation, which are crucial for maintaining emotional health. They remind you that you're not alone, reinforcing your resilience through community and shared experiences.

Another cornerstone of building resilience is **learning from setbacks.** With ADHD, setbacks might feel more pronounced, often tangled with intense emotions and a sense of personal failure. However, how you view these setbacks can significantly alter their impact on your emotional health. Instead of seeing them as failures, view them as opportunities for learning and growth. This shift in perspective reduces the fear of failure, a familiar specter for those with ADHD, and fosters a more forgiving and constructive approach to challenges. It's about acknowledging that setbacks are not stop signs but detours, perhaps rough and unexpected but still leading toward your destination.

These strategies for building emotional resilience are not just tools but investments in your emotional and psychological well-being. By integrating these practices into your life, you create a robust buffer against the natural ebb and flow of emotions that ADHD brings. Each strategy strengthens your ability to cope and thrive, enhancing your capacity to navigate life with confidence and calm. Whether through the reflective practice of journaling, the joy of hobbies, the support of structured social interactions, or the constructive reframing of setbacks, you equip yourself with the resilience needed to face the challenges of ADHD, not just with endurance but with grace and optimism.

> **Mindful Takeaway:**
>
> Find a hobby or activity that's sustainable for you to practice. Usually doing something that is scheduled and with accountability partners or friends works best. Overall, it should be enjoyable and not forced.

Mindfulness Practices for Emotional Regulation

Stepping into the world of mindfulness might feel like entering a tranquil garden; it's a space where each moment is observed, not judged, where the mind's chatter slows down, and a sense of calm prevails. For those of us with ADHD, this mental space often seems like a distant reality, as our thoughts tend to race from one idea to another, making it hard to focus or find peace. However, mindfulness offers tools to help us navigate our bustling minds, providing techniques that enhance focus, ease impulsivity, and foster emotional equilibrium.

Mindfulness, in its essence, is the practice of being fully present in the moment, aware of where we are and what we're doing, without being overly reactive or overwhelmed by what's happening around us. This might sound simple, but for someone with ADHD, it's a skill that can be life-changing. The core benefit of mindfulness for ADHD lies in its ability to anchor us in the present. This grounding can reduce the feelings of being overwhelmed that often accompany ADHD and decrease distractibility. It's about training the brain to pause before reacting, creating a space where choices can be made consciously rather than impulsively.

One of the most accessible mindfulness techniques is **guided meditation.** This practice involves listening to a recorded voice that leads you through relaxation and awareness exercises. For instance, you might be guided to focus on your breath, notice the sensations in your body, or observe your thoughts as they come and go. These sessions can vary in length, making them adaptable to your daily routine, whether you have five minutes in the morning or 20 minutes before bed. Another technique, **mindful walking,** turns a simple walk into a practice of awareness. Here, the focus is on the experience of walking—feeling the ground under your feet, noticing your breath as you move, and observing the sights and sounds around you. This can be particularly beneficial if you find sitting still challenging.

Body scans are yet another technique that can be particularly effective. This practice involves mentally scanning your body for areas of tension and consciously relaxing them. It's a way of connecting with your body, often neglected with the cognitive overload of ADHD. Starting from the toes and moving upwards, you focus on each part of the body, noticing any sensations, tension, or discomfort. This not only helps in reducing physical stress but also aids in developing a deeper awareness of the mind-body connection, which can be instrumental in managing ADHD symptoms.

The research underscores the effectiveness of these practices. Studies have shown that mindfulness meditation can reduce ADHD symptoms, particularly inattention and impulsivity. These improvements are thought to result from changes in brain function and structure associated with mindfulness practice, such as increased activity in the prefrontal cortex, an area of the brain crucial for attention and executive function. Moreover, mindfulness has been shown to enhance emotional regulation, reducing the severity of emotional reactions and improving the ability to engage in goal-directed behaviors despite emotional disruptions.

Incorporating mindfulness into your daily routine can start small. It might be as simple as practicing mindful breathing for a few minutes each day, gradually increasing the time as you become more comfortable. Over time, these moments of mindfulness can extend into other parts of your day. Suddenly, you might find yourself being mindful while doing dishes, noticing the temperature of the water and the sensation of dishes in your hands. These practices help ground your day, providing pockets of calm amidst the chaos of ADHD.

Embracing mindfulness is like planting a garden in your mind that you nurture and grow over time. The seeds are the techniques—guided meditations, mindful walking, body scans—each tool that helps cultivate a space of focus and calm within. As you nurture these seeds through regular practice, they grow into a garden that supports not just your mental health but your overall well-being, providing a refuge from the storms of ADHD. This garden does not eliminate the challenges of ADHD; instead, it offers tools to manage them more effectively, transforming how you interact with your thoughts, emotions, and the world around you.

The Impact of Stress on ADHD and How to Manage It

Stress acts like a magnifying glass on ADHD symptoms, intensifying them in ways that can feel overwhelming and sometimes unmanageable. You might notice that under stress, your typical ADHD traits, such as forgetfulness or difficulty focusing, become more pronounced, leading to a frustrating cycle where stress begets more stress. This often manifests in what can feel like a feedback loop of impulsivity and stress—stress can lead to hurried decisions or actions without full consideration, creating more chaotic situations and, consequently, more stress. Understanding this cycle is crucial because it empowers you to implement strategies specifically designed to break it, paving the way for a calmer, more controlled approach to everyday situations and unexpected challenges.

Managing stress effectively, especially for someone with ADHD, involves a combination of **time management, realistic goal-setting, and relaxation techniques**. Time management can be a significant stressor when you feel like you're constantly racing against the clock, a common scenario if you struggle to estimate how long tasks will take. Adopting techniques such as time blocking, which you might recall from our discussion on enhancing focus, can help allocate specific times for tasks, reducing the rush and panic that come from last-minute scrambles. Setting realistic goals goes hand-in-hand with effective time management. It's about aligning your expectations with your actual capacity, which involves acknowledging and planning for the ADHD-related challenges you might face. For instance, if you know that starting tasks can be complex, set a goal to initiate small parts of the task throughout the day rather than leaving it all for a last-minute push.

Relaxation techniques form another pillar of effective stress management. Techniques such as **progressive muscle relaxation,** where you tense and then relax different muscle groups, can significantly help reduce physical and mental tension. This method helps calm the body and redirects your focus away from stressors, providing a break for your mind. **Deep breathing exercises** also offer a quick, accessible way to reduce stress. Focusing on deep, controlled breathing, you engage the parasympathetic nervous system, which helps counter the body's stress response. These practices can be particularly beneficial when you feel overwhelmed as a physical reminder that you have the tools and the ability to manage your stress.

Adapting your environment to minimize stress is also crucial. This might involve organizing your living and workspace to reduce clutter, which can be a significant visual and mental distraction source. Simple changes like maintaining a clear desk, having an organized system for your paperwork, or setting up specific zones for different activities can significantly reduce stress by making your environment more manageable and less chaotic. In noisy environments, using noise-canceling headphones can help maintain your focus and keep stress at bay by shielding you from auditory distractions that can disrupt your concentration and escalate stress.

Sometimes, despite our best efforts, stress can feel too overwhelming to manage independently. This is where **professional help** can make a significant difference. Engaging with therapists or ADHD coaches who specialize in stress management can provide you with tailored strategies and support. These professionals can help you understand the specific ways in which stress affects your ADHD and work with you to develop personalized coping strategies. They can also offer guidance on implementing and sticking to the techniques discussed, ensuring that you have the knowledge and ongoing support needed to manage stress effectively.

Learning to manage stress equips you with more than just strategies to handle difficult situations. You develop a deeper understanding of how stress interacts with your ADHD and how you can take control of this dynamic to lead a more balanced, productive life. Whether through improving time management, setting achievable goals, utilizing relaxation techniques, adapting your environment, or seeking professional guidance, the goal is to create a comprehensive approach to stress that acknowledges and addresses its immediate and long-term impacts on your well-being.

Developing Empathy: Improving Relationships Through Understanding

Empathy, at its essence, is about walking in someone else's shoes, seeing through their eyes, and feeling with their heart. It's a crucial skill that enhances our connections with others, making our interactions more meaningful and compassionate. However, for those of us with ADHD, the path to empathy can sometimes be cluttered with unique challenges. The nature of ADHD can complicate how we interpret and respond to others' emotions and reactions. This doesn't mean we're any less capable of empathy; instead, it suggests that we might experience and express it differently. For instance, the impulsivity associated with ADHD might lead us to interrupt others as we eagerly respond to their stories, which could be misinterpreted as not listening or caring. Similarly, the emotional dysregulation that often accompanies ADHD can sometimes make it challenging to remain present during emotionally charged conversations as we're managing our heightened reactions.

To enhance our empathic skills, engaging in exercises such as **role-playing** can be incredibly beneficial. Through role-playing, you can practice responding to various social scenarios in a controlled, reflective manner. This helps develop a deeper understanding of different perspectives and improves your ability to regulate your responses in real-time. **Reflective listening** is another powerful exercise. It involves actively listening to the speaker and then reflecting on what you've heard, not just the words but the feelings behind them. This practice encourages deeper engagement and can significantly improve your interpersonal communications. It pushes you to focus not just on the content of the conversation but on the emotional undertones, which are often the heart of empathic interactions.

Participating in **group therapy or support groups** can also serve as a real-time practice arena for empathy. These settings often bring together individuals from diverse backgrounds, each with stories and emotional landscapes. Being part of such a group allows you to explore empathy in a multifaceted environment, where you can learn from others' experiences while sharing your own. This reciprocal exchange of understanding and support is about building empathy and enriching your social skills and emotional repertoire.

The impact of enhancing empathy on personal relationships and overall social interactions cannot be overstated. When you develop stronger empathic connections, your relationships naturally become more supportive and understanding. You're better able to sense and respond to the needs of others, which can lead to more fulfilling and harmonious interactions. Moreover, empathy can bridge the gap that ADHD sometimes creates in social settings, where misunderstandings might arise from our unique ways of processing and responding to information. By improving your empathy, you're fine-tuning your ability to communicate and connect with others, which is invaluable in personal and professional contexts.

In today's digital age, technology offers innovative ways to develop and practice empathy. For instance, digital tools and apps designed to aid in emotion recognition can be beneficial. These tools often use AI to analyze facial expressions or voice tones to identify emotions, providing real-time feedback that can help you better understand how others feel. Virtual reality (VR) simulations offer another cutting-edge tool, placing you in simulated social situations where you can practice responding to various emotional cues and scenarios. These technologies enhance your understanding of empathy and provide a safe space to practice and refine your empathic skills without the fear of real-world repercussions.

Incorporating these practices and tools into your life doesn't just enhance your ability to empathize; it transforms your interactions and relationships, providing a more profound, more nuanced way to connect with the people around you. Whether through traditional exercises like role-playing and reflective listening, engaging in group settings, or leveraging the latest digital tools, the journey to deepening your empathy is about expanding your emotional understanding and fostering more meaningful connections. This enriches your personal life and enhances your social interactions, opening up a world where relationships are built on a solid foundation of mutual understanding and respect.

Self-Compassion: Healing the ADHD Mind

Self-compassion might sound like just another wellness buzzword, but for those of us navigating life with ADHD, it's a crucial piece of the puzzle often missing. It's about treating yourself with the same kindness and understanding that you would offer a good friend. This concept is especially vital for individuals with ADHD, who often battle with persistent self-criticism and fluctuating self-esteem. ADHD can make it easy to spiral into negative self-talk, especially after a day when your symptoms have led to unfinished tasks or social missteps. Understanding and cultivating self-compassion can shift these patterns, offering a gentler way to relate to yourself, one that acknowledges challenges without judgment.

Developing self-compassion involves more than just changing how you talk to yourself; it requires integrating practices into your daily life that reinforce this mindset. Mindfulness-based self-compassion exercises are a great starting point. These practices blend the awareness-raising power of mindfulness with the nurturing perspective of compassion. One simple exercise is the Self-Compassion Break, which can be used during stress or self-doubt. It involves three steps: first, acknowledging that this is a moment of suffering; second, recognizing that suffering is a part of life shared by all humans; and third, offering yourself kindness and care in response. Phrases like "May I be kind to myself at this moment" or "I am learning and growing, and that's okay" can be mentally recited during this practice.

Self-kindness affirmations are another powerful tool. These are positive statements that you repeat to yourself to foster a compassionate self-view. Crafting affirmations that resonate with your specific experiences with ADHD can be particularly effective. For instance, after a day where distractibility has prevailed, you might remind yourself, "I am more than my distractions," or "Each moment is a new opportunity to focus." These affirmations can be used daily or whenever you are caught in a whirlwind of self-criticism.

The benefits of developing self-compassion are profound. Research has shown that self-compassion can lead to significant decreases in anxiety and depression, which are often comorbid with ADHD. It enhances emotional well-being by shifting how you relate to yourself—from a critical stance to a supportive one. This shift can reduce the stress that often accompanies ADHD symptoms as you begin to view these challenges through a lens of understanding and patience rather than frustration and disappointment. Additionally, self-compassion can improve motivation, encouraging you to see setbacks as learning opportunities rather than failures.

Incorporating self-compassion into therapeutic practices can also amplify the benefits of traditional ADHD treatments. For example, when therapists integrate self-compassion into their sessions, they help clients address their symptoms and relate to them in a healthier way. This integrated approach can be particularly practical in therapy settings, where individuals are encouraged to explore and transform their relationships with their thoughts and emotions. Discussing self-compassion openly in therapy sessions and practicing compassion-focused exercises can equip you with tools to maintain this perspective beyond the therapist's office.

By embracing self-compassion, you're not just managing ADHD symptoms; you're nurturing a relationship with yourself rooted in kindness and understanding. This approach does not eliminate the challenges of ADHD, but it does change how you experience and respond to these challenges. It allows for a gentler journey through the ups and downs, providing a compassionate anchor that can hold you steady, even on difficult days. As we wrap up this chapter on emotional intelligence and resilience, the tools and insights shared here are more than strategies; they're invitations to transform your relationship with yourself and, by extension, your ADHD. These practices aren't just about coping; they're about thriving and fostering a compassionate inner dialogue that supports your growth and well-being every step. As we move forward, remember that each step in this journey builds upon the last, crafting a life that celebrates all parts of you, ADHD included.

> **Terms & Techniques:**
>
> **4-4-8 technique:** breathe in for 4 seconds, hold for 4 seconds, exhale for 8 seconds
>
> **Cognitive Behavioral Therapy (CBT):** therapy where you identify and change unhelpful thought patterns that can trigger or worsen emotional distress
>
> **Emotional Resilence:** capacity to bounce back from difficulties and manage life's ups and downs effectively
>
> **Mindfulness:** the practice of being fully present in the moment, aware of where we are and what we're doing, without being overly reactive or overwhelmed by what's happening around us
>
> **Empathy:** walking in someone else's shoes, seeing through their eyes, and feeling with their heart
>
> **Self-Compassion:** treating yourself with the same kindness and understanding that you would offer a good friend

Make a Difference with Your Review

Unlock the Power of Generosity

"Helping one person might not change the whole world, but it could change the world for one person." - Anonymous

People who give without expecting anything in return live longer, happier lives and often achieve more success. So, during our time together, I want to make a positive impact.

To make that happen, I have a question for you...

Would you help someone you've never met, even if you never got credit for it?

Who is this person, you ask? They are like you. Or, at least, like you used to be. They want to improve, make a difference, and need guidance but aren't sure where to find it.

Our mission is to make understanding and mastering executive functioning skills learning accessible to everyone. And the only way for me to accomplish that mission is by reaching…well...everyone.

This is where you come in. Most people do, in fact, judge a book by its cover (and its reviews). So here's my ask on behalf of a struggling adult with ADHD you've never met:

Please help that person by leaving this book a review.

Your gift costs no money and takes less than 60 seconds, but it can change a fellow reader's life forever. Your review could help...

...one more person manage their day better.

...one more adult feel less overwhelmed.

...one more employee succeed at work.

...one more person build better relationships.

...one more dream come true.

To get that 'feel good' feeling and help this person for real, all you have to do is...and it takes less than 60 seconds...

leave a review.

Simply use the QR code below:

If you feel good about helping a faceless reader, you are my kind of person. Welcome to the club. You're one of us.

I'm that much more excited to help you master executive functioning skills faster and easier than you can possibly imagine. You'll love the tips and strategies I'm about to share in the coming chapters.

Thank you from the bottom of my heart. Now, back to our regularly scheduled programming.

- Cheering you on, Sharon Banks

PS - Fun fact: If you provide something of value to another person, it makes you more valuable to them. If you'd like to spread goodwill straight from another reader - and you believe this book will help them - send this book their way.

STRATEGY #4
BUILDING AND MAINTAINING RELATIONSHIPS

You're at a party filled with conversations and laughter. People exchange stories and insights, but you find yourself nodding without hearing what's being said. Your mind races through thoughts about what you should say next or drifts to a comment someone made earlier that you can't seem to shake off. This scenario might resonate deeply if you're navigating adult life with ADHD, where communication isn't just about speaking or listening but managing a whirlwind of thoughts and emotions that demand your attention simultaneously.

Communication Skills for Adults with ADHD

Effective communication is like a dance that requires rhythm and coordination, and when ADHD is in the mix, keeping up with the steps can feel daunting. Common challenges such as interrupting others mid-conversation, forgetting crucial details, or drifting off during discussions can strain even the strongest relationships. These issues stem not from a lack of care or respect but from the way ADHD influences your brain's wiring and functioning. The good news? With the proper techniques, you can become a more skilled and confident communicator, turning potential misunderstandings into opportunities for deeper connection.

Understanding ADHD Communication Challenges

The first step in honing your communication skills is understanding the specific hurdles that ADHD introduces. One of the most common is the tendency to interrupt others. This often happens because the brain with ADHD is constantly buzzing with thoughts and ideas that feel urgent, pushing you to voice them before they're forgotten. Similarly, difficulty with listening closely in conversations can arise, not from disinterest but from being easily distracted by background noise or internal thoughts, making it hard to stay engaged. Another common challenge is remembering key details, which can lead to clarity and satisfaction in personal and professional interactions. Recognizing these patterns is crucial for self-awareness and fostering patience and compassion towards yourself and others.

Active Listening Techniques

Active listening is a powerful skill that can dramatically improve your interactions. It involves fully concentrating on what is being said rather than passively hearing the speaker's message. **Reflective listening**, a core component of active listening, is particularly effective. This technique involves paraphrasing the speaker's words to confirm understanding and demonstrate empathy. For instance, if a friend tells you about a stressful day at work, you might respond with, "It sounds like you had a tough day and felt overwhelmed by the workload." This not only shows that you're paying attention but also that you care about their feelings, enhancing the emotional connection.

Clarity in Expression

Expressing yourself clearly and effectively is another critical aspect of communication. For adults with ADHD, thoughts can often feel scattered, which makes coherent expression challenging. *One helpful strategy is to pause briefly during conversation to organize your thoughts.* This might initially feel awkward, but it allows you to gather your thoughts and communicate more deliberately. Additionally, before entering a discussion or meeting, outline your main points or questions in advance. This preparation can reduce anxiety about forgetting important points and help you contribute more effectively to the conversation.

Utilizing Visual Aids

Visual aids can be a game-changer in improving communication for adults with ADHD. They help structure your thoughts and provide cues to keep the conversation on track. For instance, in a work setting, using notes or diagrams during presentations can help you convey complex information more clearly and keep track of your points. In personal settings, **jotting down key points** you want to discuss in a notebook before a serious conversation can ensure you cover all the topics you intend to without getting sidetracked. Visual aids not only assist in organizing your thoughts but also in making them more accessible and understandable to others, enhancing both the clarity and effectiveness of your communication.

By embracing these strategies, you can navigate the complexities of communication with greater confidence and skill. Whether practicing active listening to deepen your relationships, using pauses to enhance clarity, or incorporating visual aids to help organize your thoughts, each step you take builds on your ability to connect and communicate more effectively. Remember, effective communication is not about perfection but about genuine efforts to understand and be understood, creating opportunities for more prosperous, more rewarding interactions. As you continue to develop these skills, you likely find that your conversations become more fulfilling, and your relationships are strengthened and enriched by a deeper understanding and mutual respect.

> **Communication Take-Aways:**
>
> • Be self-aware when you interrupt others and pay attention to key details in the conversation
>
> • Practice active listening: paraphrase the speaker's words to show understanding and empathy
>
> • Pause briefly to organize your thoughts
>
> • Jot down key points you want to share – visual aids are helpful to have when communicating

Navigating Relationships at Work with ADHD

Navigating the intricate landscape of professional relationships when you have ADHD can often feel like you're trying to speak a language you're only partly fluent in. Every workplace has its dynamics, and when ADHD is part of your reality, these dynamics can sometimes seem amplified. One of the most sensitive aspects of managing ADHD in a professional setting is the decision to disclose your diagnosis. This decision is deeply personal and can have significant implications for how you're perceived and the support you might receive.

Disclosing your ADHD to your employer or colleagues can feel daunting. There's the fear of being labeled, misunderstood, or even discriminated against. However, sharing your diagnosis can also lead to a better understanding from your peers and superiors and access to accommodations that can significantly improve your productivity and job satisfaction. If you choose to disclose, it's crucial to do so strategically. Consider the culture of your workplace; is there a general openness to diversity and inclusion? Gauge the attitudes of your superiors or HR department towards mental health and neurodiversity. When you decide to disclose, frame it within the context of how understanding your ADHD can benefit your team's dynamics and productivity rather than just listing its challenges.

Creating an ADHD-friendly work environment is another crucial step in navigating professional relationships. This involves negotiating for flexible working hours if your productivity peaks at non-traditional times. Or you may need a quieter workspace away from the hum and buzz of an open-plan office. Be bold when discussing these needs with your employer. Most will appreciate your proactive approach and willingness to find solutions that enhance your work performance. Remember, the goal is to create a work environment where you can thrive, not just survive.

Building and maintaining professionalism in the workplace is also key. This means managing time effectively and meeting deadlines, skills that can sometimes be challenging if you have ADHD. Develop systems that help you stay on top of your tasks, like using digital tools to keep track of deadlines or setting meeting reminders. Time management isn't just about keeping track of your tasks—it's also about prioritizing them effectively so that you're always aware of what needs your attention most urgently. Additionally, work on being present in meetings and interactions with colleagues. This can be challenging when your mind buzzes with a million other thoughts, but practicing mindfulness can help you stay focused and engaged.

Handling criticism is another aspect of professional interactions that can be particularly challenging. It's natural to feel defensive when you receive negative feedback, especially when you're already managing the internal critiques that often come with ADHD. However, learning to view feedback as a tool for growth rather than a personal attack can change how you respond to it. When receiving criticism, try to listen actively and ask clarifying questions. This can help ensure that you understand the feedback fully and can address it in a constructive manner. Reflect on the feedback privately, parsing out actionable items from comments that may be influenced by misunderstandings about your work style.

Navigating professional relationships when you have ADHD involves a delicate balance of self-awareness, proactive communication, and strategic adjustments to your work environment. By understanding and articulating your needs, you can foster a work atmosphere that acknowledges your unique challenges and celebrates your distinctive strengths. Whether through open dialogue about your needs, creating systems for enhanced productivity, or handling feedback with grace, each step you take is about crafting a professional identity that respects both your challenges and your capabilities. In doing so, you make your work life more manageable and model for others the importance of understanding and accommodating neurodiversity in the workplace.

> **Mindful Take-Away:**
>
> It's always your choice whether to disclose that you have ADHD. Talk to HR to see if there are existing initiatives in place for your specific needs with ADHD and how you are protected in your job in case of questionable situations where you should have been accommodated.

Managing Conflict with Emotional Intelligence

Conflicts in personal relationships, professional settings, or even internal struggles can often feel like navigating a treacherous storm. For those of us with ADHD, the quick shifts in emotion and the impulsivity that sometimes accompanies our interactions can make these waters particularly choppy. Understanding what triggers these conflicts is the first step in learning to navigate them with emotional intelligence. For many of us, these triggers could be as simple as a change in routine, perceived criticism, or sensory overload, which can unexpectedly heighten our emotional responses. Recognizing these triggers involves a mix of self-reflection and mindfulness; it's about tracking your reactions and identifying patterns over time. Keeping a journal can be helpful in this process, allowing you to log incidents that stir up strong emotions and reflect on what might have sparked them. This ongoing log provides a clearer picture, helping you anticipate and prepare for situations that might lead to conflicts.

Once you know your triggers, adopting effective conflict resolution techniques can significantly change how you handle potential clashes. One such technique is **the 'STOP' method**—Stop, Think, Observe, Proceed when you feel a conflict brewing, first stop. This pause is crucial as it prevents the knee-jerk reactions that often escalate conflicts. Next, think about what you're upset about. Is it the situation at hand, or is something deeper at play? Then, observe. Pay attention to not only what the other person is saying but also their body language and your physiological responses. Are your hands clenched? Is your heart racing? Recognizing these signs can help you gauge the intensity of your reaction and decide how best to proceed. Finally, proceed with a response that addresses the issue rather than your emotional reaction to it. This method doesn't just apply to external conflicts; it's equally effective for internal ones, where you might struggle with self-criticism or indecision.

Maintaining emotional control during conflicts is another critical aspect of managing them effectively. Techniques such as deep breathing exercises can be invaluable here. Deep breathing helps in reducing the physiological reactions associated with stress and anger, such as an increased heart rate or rapid breathing. Focusing on taking slow, deep breaths can help calm your mind and body, making it easier to respond to the situation with a more evident, more composed mindset. Another helpful practice is to take a brief timeout if you feel overwhelmed. This could mean stepping away from the situation or simply closing your eyes for a few moments to regather your thoughts. The key is to give yourself a moment to detach from the immediate emotional responses and to consider a more measured approach to the conflict.

Learning from conflicts, rather than just getting through them, can transform these experiences from hurdles to stepping stones. Each conflict presents an opportunity to understand how you interact with the world around you. Reflect on each incident after it has passed, and consider what you might have learned about your triggers, your communication style, and how you handle stress. This reflection can be transformative, offering insights that help you handle future conflicts better and deepen your understanding of yourself and your relationships. By framing conflicts as opportunities for growth, you foster a mindset that values personal development and continuous learning, which are invaluable for anyone, especially for adults navigating life with ADHD.

Navigating conflicts with emotional intelligence is not about avoiding disagreements or suppressing your feelings. It's about understanding your emotional triggers, employing strategies to manage reactions healthily, and learning from each experience to improve your handling of future conflicts. This approach doesn't just resolve disputes; it builds stronger, more resilient relationships and a deeper understanding of yourself. As you continue to apply these strategies, you might find that what once seemed like overwhelming storms become manageable challenges, each offering valuable lessons and opportunities for growth.

The "STOP" method

1.STOP – pause to prevent reactive actions

2.THINK – think what you're upset about. Is it the situation, or something deeper?

3.OBSERVE – Pay attention to what the other person is saying and their body language and also your physiological reactions

4.PROCEED – proceed with a response that addresses the issue rather than your emotional reaction to it

Building Support Networks: Finding Your Community

Discovering a sense of belonging and understanding through a strong support network can profoundly impact your life, especially when navigating the complexities of adult ADHD. Picture this: a space where you're not just heard but understood. You can share your struggles and victories without fear of judgment. This is what a robust support network offers—emotional backing, practical advice, and a community that truly gets it. These networks become your tribe, providing a foundational support system that can help stabilize the often-turbulent experiences associated with ADHD.

The benefits of such networks are multifaceted. Emotionally, they offer a haven where you can express your feelings and frustrations, knowing you're not alone in your experiences. Practically, members of your support network can share strategies that have worked for them, from managing time effectively to handling emotional dysregulation, providing you with a toolkit of approaches that might be effective in your situation. Moreover, feeling part of a community can significantly enhance your sense of belonging and self-esteem. It's a powerful reminder that your challenges are part of a shared human experience, not a reflection of personal failure.

Finding the right support group that aligns with your needs and experiences can sometimes feel like searching for a needle in a haystack. Start by exploring local and online options. Many communities have ADHD support groups where members meet regularly to discuss their challenges and successes. Online forums and social media groups can also be invaluable if in-person options are limited. Platforms like Reddit and Facebook host various ADHD support groups where you can connect with others from the comfort of your home. When choosing a group, consider the tone and activity level of the discussions—does it feel supportive and positive? Are the conversations constructive? You might need to try several groups before finding one where you feel at home.

Once you've found a group that feels right, active participation is the key to reaping the full benefits. Engage in discussions, share your own experiences, and offer support to others. Active involvement helps you gain more insights and support and strengthens your connections within the group, building more profound, more meaningful relationships. These connections can become significant sources of support and encouragement, people who can offer practical advice and emotional understanding exactly when needed.

Leveraging social media responsibly is another aspect of building your support network. Social platforms can be double-edged swords—they provide valuable connections and resources but can also lead to overstimulation or distractions. To use social media effectively, set clear boundaries for yourself. Allocate specific times of the day for social media and stick to platforms that offer the most support for your ADHD challenges. Tools like timers or apps that limit social media use can help manage your time online, preventing you from falling down the rabbit hole of endless scrolling. Remember, the goal of using social media should be to enhance your support network, not to replace real connections with virtual ones.

In building your support network, remember that the strength of your connections often reflects the quality of your engagement. By choosing the right groups, participating actively, and using social media wisely, you create a supportive community that not only understands the challenges of ADHD but also celebrates the unique perspectives and strengths you bring to the table. This network, your tribe, becomes a powerful ally in your journey, offering the tools, understanding, and encouragement needed to navigate ADHD with confidence and resilience.

Love and ADHD: Maintaining Romantic Relationships

Navigating romantic relationships when you have ADHD can sometimes feel like you're constantly dancing to a tune that changes tempo without warning. The characteristics of ADHD, such as impulsivity, forgetfulness, and emotional dysregulation, can indeed introduce unique challenges to relationships. Perhaps you've found yourself forgetting important dates like anniversaries, or your emotional responses have been more intense than the situation warranted. These moments can create misunderstandings or friction between partners. However, understanding and openly addressing these challenges can transform potential stumbling blocks into stepping stones for a stronger, more understanding relationship.

Impulsivity might lead to spontaneous decisions without discussing them with your partner, which might be exciting but can also lead to feelings of exclusion or instability. On the other hand, forgetfulness might come off as inattentiveness to your partner's needs or desires, whether forgetting to pick up something on your way home or missing a date night. Emotional dysregulation can further complicate interactions, making it difficult to remain composed during disagreements or to express your feelings appropriately. Each of these aspects can strain your connection, but they also offer opportunities for growth and deeper understanding.

Open communication is the keystone of any healthy relationship, and this holds especially true when ADHD is in the mix. Fostering an environment where both partners can speak openly and honestly about their feelings, needs, and frustrations is vital. This might involve setting aside specific times to check in with each other, free from distractions, where you can talk about how things are going in your relationship. During these discussions, try to speak clearly about your experiences without making assumptions about your partner's intentions or feelings. Consider shared digital calendars or reminder systems for important dates and agreements if forgetfulness is a challenge. When emotions run high, use tactics like taking a short break to collect your thoughts or expressing your feelings through writing if verbal communication is too intense.

Collaborative planning is another powerful tool in strengthening relationships when ADHD is involved. This involves making decisions together, from daily plans to more significant life choices, ensuring both partners have input and feel valued. This can be particularly helpful in balancing the spontaneity that often comes with ADHD and the need for relationship stability and predictability. For instance, while planning a vacation, one partner could handle booking accommodations while the other plans activities. Regular planning meetings help both partners feel more engaged and in control of their shared life. These meetings can also be an excellent time to address any concerns about forgotten responsibilities or discuss strategies to handle them better.

Couples therapy that focuses on ADHD can also be a transformative experience. Such therapy provides a structured environment where both partners can learn about the impact of ADHD on their relationship. A therapist who understands ADHD can offer valuable insights and tools tailored to your situation. They can help you develop strategies to manage ADHD symptoms that affect your relationship and improve communication and problem-solving skills. Therapy can also be a safe space to explore sensitive topics that might be difficult to address alone.

Navigating romantic relationships with ADHD involves understanding the unique challenges it brings, communicating openly, planning collaboratively, and sometimes seeking professional guidance. These strategies not only help manage the symptoms of ADHD but also create a supportive, loving relationship where both partners feel understood and valued.

From tackling impulsivity and forgetfulness to enhancing communication and collaborative planning, the strategies discussed aim to fortify partnerships against the challenges posed by ADHD. As we transition into the next chapter, we'll explore lifestyle adjustments that can further aid in managing ADHD in daily life, ensuring that each step is one towards a more balanced, fulfilling personal and professional life.

Road to better relationships:

Active listening: fully concentrating on what is being said rather than passively hearing the speaker's message

Reflective Listening: This technique involves paraphrasing the speaker's words to confirm understanding and demonstrate empathy

The "STOP" method: Stop, Think, Observe, Proceed when you feel a conflict brewing

Finding your community: build a network where you can share your struggles and victories

STRATEGY #5
LIFESTYLE ADJUSTMENTS FOR ADHD MANAGEMENT

Imagine you're planting a garden. You know that the soil's quality, the amount of sunlight, and the water it receives all play pivotal roles in how well your plants will thrive. Now, think of your body as that garden and the food you eat as the inputs that can either nourish or fail to nourish it. For those of us navigating life with ADHD, understanding the profound impact of diet on our symptoms is like discovering the best fertilizer mix for our garden—essential for growth and resilience.

Nutrition and ADHD: Foods That Help and Foods to Avoid

Impact of Diet on ADHD

The connection between what we eat and how we feel is well-documented, but for those with ADHD, this relationship takes on even greater significance. Certain foods can exacerbate symptoms, while others help alleviate them. It's all about the brain-gut axis, an often-overlooked pathway that plays a critical role in mood regulation and cognitive function. The neurotransmitters responsible for keeping our brain ticking—including dopamine, which is crucial for focus and motivation—are synthesized in the gut. So, if your gut isn't at its healthiest, it can directly impact the levels of these neurotransmitters, thereby affecting your ADHD symptoms.

Think about how you feel after a heavy, greasy meal compared to a light, nutritious one. The difference isn't just in your stomach; it's in your brain, too. Foods high in simple carbohydrates and sugars can cause spikes and crashes in blood sugar levels, which may lead to fluctuations in energy and mood, exacerbating the highs and lows that many with ADHD experience. On the other hand, a balanced diet rich in complex carbohydrates, proteins, and healthy fats can provide a more stable energy source, allowing for better overall control of ADHD symptoms.

Beneficial Foods

So, what does an ADHD-friendly diet look like? First, it's rich in **omega-3 fatty acids** found in foods like salmon, flaxseeds, and walnuts. These fats are not just good for your heart; they play a crucial role in brain function, helping to manage mood swings and improve cognitive function. Protein is another key player. It helps to balance blood sugar levels and provides the amino acids needed to synthesize neurotransmitters. Incorporating protein sources like chicken, beans, and eggs throughout the day can help keep your energy levels steady and your mind alert.

Complex carbohydrates are also beneficial. They break down more slowly in the body, providing a steady energy source without the spikes and crashes associated with simple sugars. Foods like **whole grains, fruits, and vegetables** are excellent sources of complex carbs, plus they're packed with vitamins and minerals that support overall brain health.

Foods to Limit or Avoid

Conversely, there are certain foods and additives that those with ADHD should limit or avoid. Top of the list are artificial colorings and certain preservatives, which studies have shown can increase hyperactivity in children with ADHD. While the research on adults continues, it's prudent to be cautious about these additives.

High-sugar foods and simple carbohydrates, like those found in cakes, cookies, and white bread, can also be problematic. They might give you a quick burst of energy, but this is often followed by a sharp drop in blood sugar, leaving you tired and irritable. Caffeine and alcohol can also complicate ADHD symptoms, affecting sleep and mood, so moderation is key.

Creating an ADHD-Friendly Diet Plan

Transitioning to an ADHD-friendly diet doesn't have to be overwhelming. Start small. Introduce one new healthy food a week, and experiment with recipes that incorporate these beneficial ingredients. Planning your meals can also be incredibly helpful, reducing the likelihood of reaching for convenient but less healthy options when you're hungry and rushed.

Keep a food diary for a few weeks. Note what you eat and how you feel afterward. This can help you identify patterns and pinpoint foods that might be problematic or beneficial for you. Remember, the goal here isn't perfection. It's about making gradual changes that can lead to more significant improvements in managing your ADHD.

Incorporating a balanced, nutrient-rich diet is like laying a solid foundation for your garden. It won't eliminate ADHD, but it can significantly mitigate the symptoms, helping you to feel more in control and ready to grow. As you adjust your diet and notice changes, remember that this is just one part of a broader strategy to manage ADHD. Each positive change you make builds on the last, contributing to a healthier, more balanced lifestyle.

> **Nutrition Tips:**
>
> • Focus on omega-3 fatty acid foods like salmon, walnuts, and flaxseed
>
> • Eat more complex carbs to give a steady source of energy, such as, whole grains, fruits, and vegetables
>
> • Limit and avoid high-sugar foods and simple carbohydrates, caffeine, and alcohol. Moderation is key.

The Role of Exercise in Managing ADHD

Imagine feeling more focused, calmer, and energized, with a sense of achievement at the end of the day. It sounds appealing. Well, stepping into a routine that includes regular exercise can help bring this vision to life, especially for those of us navigating the ups and downs of ADHD. Engaging in physical activity is not just about improving physical health; it has profound benefits for mental well-being, particularly in managing symptoms of ADHD such as restlessness, difficulty concentrating, and mood fluctuations.

Exercise acts like a natural stimulant for the brain, akin to a cup of morning coffee but without the caffeine jitters. When you engage in physical activity, your brain releases several neurotransmitters, including dopamine, norepinephrine, and serotonin, which are crucial in regulating mood and attention. These are the same neurotransmitters that are targeted by common ADHD medications. Regular exercise can help increase the baseline levels of these neurotransmitters, naturally helping to improve focus, lift mood, and reduce impulsivity. Moreover, physical movement helps burn off excess energy and tension, leading to improved sleep patterns and decreased anxiety, which are often areas of struggle for those with ADHD.

When considering the types of exercise that are particularly beneficial for ADHD, variety is critical. Aerobic activities like running, cycling, or swimming are fantastic because they increase heart rate and promote the release of endorphins, creating a 'runner's high' that can last well beyond the workout. These activities can help clear the mental fog that often accompanies ADHD. On days when you're feeling agitated or when your mind won't stop racing, engaging in these vigorous activities can provide a much-needed reset, bringing a sense of calm and clarity.

Team sports are another excellent option. They offer the dual benefits of physical exercise and social interaction, which can be therapeutic for those who often feel isolated due to their ADHD symptoms. Sports such as soccer, basketball, or even group classes at the gym provide structured social settings where you can connect with others in a dynamic, supportive environment. The rules and cooperation required in team sports also encourage the development of discipline and focus, skills that can be beneficial in daily life with ADHD.

Yoga deserves a special mention. Unlike more intense aerobic activities, yoga combines physical movement with breath control and meditation, promoting a sense of inner peace and mindfulness that can be particularly beneficial for emotional regulation—one of the areas often affected by ADHD. The practice encourages a focus on the present moment, helping to combat the distractibility that plagues those with ADHD. It's also highly adaptable; regardless of your fitness level, you can find a style of yoga that feels comfortable yet challenging.

Incorporating exercise into your daily routine might seem daunting, especially when you struggle with time management or maintaining consistent habits, common challenges in ADHD. Starting small can make a significant difference. Schedule short workouts, perhaps 10-15 minutes long, and gradually increase the duration as it becomes a more integral part of your routine. Choosing activities that you genuinely enjoy is crucial. If you love being outdoors, opt for a jog in the park over a treadmill. If music energizes you, perhaps a dance class could be more engaging than a silent yoga session. The key is to make exercise something you look forward to, not another chore.

Overcoming barriers to regular exercise, like lack of motivation or boredom, can be tackled by setting clear, achievable goals and tracking your progress. Celebrate each small victory, whether it's running a bit longer than last time, mastering a new yoga pose, or simply sticking to your schedule for the week. For those days when motivation is low, focus on the benefits you've noticed, perhaps improved focus at work or better sleep. Remember, every bit of movement counts, and consistency is more beneficial than intensity. Adjust your mindset to view exercise as a regular part of self-care, a non-negotiable appointment that holds the same importance as any other commitment in your life.

Incorporating regular physical activity into your life isn't just about enhancing fitness; it's a vital strategy for managing ADHD. By engaging in a mix of aerobic exercises, team sports, and mindfulness practices like yoga, you not only improve your physical health but also enhance your mental clarity, emotional stability, and overall quality of life. As you lace up your sneakers or roll out your yoga mat, you're taking a powerful step towards not just managing but thriving with ADHD.

Sleep Hygiene Practices for Better ADHD Management

Imagine lying in bed, your mind racing with thoughts from the day or plans for tomorrow while the clock ticks away silently. For many of us with ADHD, this scenario is all too familiar. Sleep, which should be a restful escape, becomes yet another battleground where our symptoms seem to have strengthened rather than subdued. The intricate dance between ADHD and sleep is complex, as each negatively impacts the other. Poor sleep exacerbates ADHD symptoms, which, in turn, can lead to even worse sleep. Understanding this cycle is the first step towards breaking it.

ADHD often brings with it an array of sleep disturbances, from trouble falling asleep and staying asleep to restless legs syndrome and sleep apnea. These issues stem from the same neurological quirks that lead to daytime symptoms. Our brains, particularly the parts that regulate sleep and attention, are constantly firing in sometimes unhelpful patterns. For instance, the delayed sleep phase syndrome, which is common in the ADHD community, shifts the natural sleep cycle to a later time, making it difficult to fall asleep and wake up at socially accepted times. This misalignment can lead to a significant sleep deficit, affecting everything from mood and cognitive function to overall health.

Addressing these issues starts with establishing robust sleep hygiene practices. The cornerstone of good sleep hygiene is consistency. Going to bed and waking up at the same time every day helps regulate your body's internal clock, which can ease the process of falling asleep and waking up. This might sound like a monumental task if your schedule is unpredictable, but even small efforts, like adjusting your bedtime to the same 15 minutes each night, can make a significant difference.

Creating a restful environment is equally important. Your bedroom should be a sanctuary that signals to your brain that it's time to wind down. Consider the comfort of your mattress and pillows, the light levels, and the temperature. A cool, dark, and quiet room often promotes better sleep. If you live in a noisy area or find complete silence unsettling, a white noise machine or a fan can provide a soothing backdrop that masks disruptive sounds. Additionally, investing in blackout curtains can help keep your room dark, especially if you're sensitive to light, which can be a significant sleep disruptor for those with ADHD.

For many of us with ADHD, our minds don't simply shut off when our heads hit the pillow. This is where mindfulness and relaxation techniques can be invaluable. Practices such as guided imagery, progressive muscle relaxation, or deep breathing exercises can help calm a racing mind and prepare your body for sleep. Integrating these practices into your bedtime routine can signal to your body that it's time to slow down, easing the transition into sleep.

Tools and Resources for Better Sleep

Navigating sleep with ADHD often requires more than just good habits; sometimes, we need tools that align with our specific needs. Sleep tracking apps, for instance, can provide insights into your sleep patterns, helping you understand how well you're sleeping and identify potential areas for improvement. These apps can monitor everything from your sleep duration to the quality of your sleep cycles, offering data that can be incredibly enlightening if you're trying to figure out what's keeping you up at night.

Weighted blankets have also gained popularity, particularly among those with ADHD, for their soothing effects. The gentle pressure they provide can mimic the feeling of being hugged, which can be comforting and may help reduce anxiety and sensory overload, making it easier to fall asleep.

For those who struggle with the sensory aspects of ADHD at night, whether it's the feeling of sheets or the sound of a partner's breathing, consider personalized adjustments. Use hypoallergic materials for your bedding or wear earplugs to mitigate noise disturbances. Each small adjustment, tailored to your specific sensitivities, can contribute significantly to a better night's sleep.

Sleep is not merely a pause in our daily lives but a vital foundation for our well-being, especially so for those of us with ADHD. By understanding the unique challenges ADHD presents at night and adopting tailored sleep hygiene practices, you can transform your experience with sleep from a nightly challenge to a restorative escape. Remember, improving your sleep quality is a gradual process, and small, consistent changes can lead to significant improvements. Embrace these practices not just as routines but as acts of self-care that honor your body's needs, paving the way for more peaceful nights and vibrant mornings.

Organizing Your Space: Tips for Clutter Control

Imagine stepping into a room where every item has a place, the surfaces are clear, and you feel a wave of calm wash over you. This isn't just a daydream for those of us with ADHD; it's a possible reality that can dramatically influence how we feel and function. Clutter, on the other hand, isn't just an eyesore—it's a significant source of stress and a common culprit behind decreased productivity, especially for individuals with ADHD. The chaos of a cluttered space can mirror the chaos in our minds, making it tougher to focus and process information efficiently.

The impact of clutter is more profound than one might think. In a cluttered environment, the constant visual reminders of disorganization can trigger stress and anxiety. This is particularly challenging for those of us with ADHD, as we can become easily overwhelmed by too many stimuli, leading to sensory overload. Moreover, clutter can sap our energy and motivation. The task of having to sort through piles just to find what you need or clear a space to work can be daunting enough to put off tasks altogether, feeding into the cycle of procrastination that many with ADHD struggle with.

Tackling clutter requires a strategic approach, and the first step is effective decluttering. Start with one small area—this could be a desk, a drawer, or even a section of a room. The key is to not overwhelm yourself with the task of decluttering an entire house all at once. Break it down into manageable, bite-sized pieces. Sort items into categories: keep, donate, discard, or relocate. Be decisive. If you haven't used something in over a year, it's likely you don't need it. This process can be liberating, as each item you choose to discard or donate can feel like lifting a little weight off your shoulders.

Regular maintenance is crucial. Once you've decluttered, set up a weekly routine to go through your spaces to ensure that everything is in its rightful place and that new clutter isn't forming. This might seem like a chore, but regular maintenance can actually become a calming ritual, a way to exert control over your environment and, by extension, over some aspects of your ADHD.

In terms of organizational tools and systems, there are plenty to choose from, and finding the right ones can make a world of difference. Labeling is a simple yet effective way to keep things organized. Whether it's labeling drawers, bins, folders, or digital files, labels can help ensure that every item has a designated home and can be easily found when needed.

Storage solutions such as drawer dividers, shelves, and desk organizers can also help keep your physical space tidy and functional. For digital clutter, consider using digital organization apps that can help manage electronic files and reduce the stress of dealing with digital overloads, such as cloud storage services or document management systems.

Personalizing your space is not just about aesthetics; it's about creating an environment that supports your productivity and reflects your personal style. This can significantly enhance your comfort and efficiency. Choose colors and decorations that you find uplifting and calming. If you love nature, incorporate elements like plants or nature-themed artwork. If you find certain scents relaxing, consider using aroma diffusers. Personal touches will make your space more inviting and comforting, encouraging you to spend time there and stay productive.

By understanding the impact of clutter, implementing effective decluttering strategies, using organizational tools, and personalizing your space, you can create an environment that not only supports your efforts to manage ADHD but also enhances your overall quality of life. This transformed space can become a sanctuary where clarity and productivity thrive, helping you navigate the daily challenges of ADHD with greater ease and confidence.

Balancing Leisure and Responsibilities

Navigating the delicate balance between work, responsibilities, and leisure can often feel like trying to keep plates spinning on poles. For those of us with ADHD, where distraction and time management can be daily challenges, maintaining this balance is not just beneficial—it's vital for our mental health and overall well-being. Understandably, when responsibilities pile up, leisure might be the first thing we sacrifice. However, leisure isn't just downtime. It's a critical component of a balanced life, offering a necessary respite for our often overstimulated minds and providing a space for creativity and relaxation that can rejuvenate our mental energy.

Prioritizing effectively between what needs to be done and what you wish to do for enjoyment requires a nuanced approach, especially when both seem equally pressing. One practical technique is the "Must, Should, Could" method. Start by categorizing your tasks and activities into three groups: 'Must' for tasks that are urgent and important, 'Should' for tasks that are important but not urgent, and 'Could' for tasks that are neither urgent nor important but are enjoyable or fulfilling. This method helps in visualizing and organizing your day or week, allowing you to see where your 'Could' activities, or leisure times, can fit in without compromising your responsibilities. It's about giving yourself permission to enjoy life while keeping up with the demands that come with it.

Integrating leisure activities into your daily life, especially when schedules feel packed to the brim, might seem like a luxury you can't afford. Yet, it's these activities that often provide the energy and mood boost needed to enhance productivity in other areas of your life. Start small; it could be as simple as reading a book for ten minutes, taking a short walk, or meditating between work tasks. These brief periods of leisure can serve as effective breaks, mentally refreshing you and enhancing your focus when you return to work-related tasks. For instance, consider the Pomodoro Technique, where work is broken down into intervals traditionally 25 minutes long, separated by five-minute breaks. These breaks are perfect opportunities to engage in a quick leisure activity, like sketching or playing a musical instrument, which can help clear your mind and reduce feelings of being overwhelmed.

Setting clear boundaries is crucial for ensuring that work doesn't seep into your leisure time, a common issue for those of us with ADHD who might struggle with impulsivity and time management. Establishing and maintaining these boundaries can be as straightforward as setting alarms to begin and end tasks or physically separating work areas from relaxation areas in your home. Communicate these boundaries clearly with others, whether it's family members or colleagues, so they can support you in maintaining them. For example, if you decide post-6 PM is your designated family or relaxation time, let your coworkers know you won't respond to emails during these hours. This not only helps in managing expectations but also aids in making your off-time truly yours, allowing you to recharge fully.

Remember, balancing work and leisure is not about allocating equal time to each but about ensuring that each has its rightful place in your life, contributing to your overall happiness and functionality. By prioritizing effectively, integrating leisure activities into your routine, and setting firm boundaries around your time, you can create a more balanced, fulfilling life. This balance isn't just beneficial; it's essential for managing ADHD symptoms and enhancing your ability to perform well across all areas of life. Embrace these strategies as part of your ongoing adaptation to life with ADHD, where the ultimate goal is not just to survive but to thrive.

Daily Formula for a healthy lifestyle:

- Healthy diet
- Physical activity and exercise
- Sleep hygiene
- Decluttered spaces
- Balance with leisure and responsibilities

Travel and ADHD: Strategies for Smooth Adventures

Traveling can be an exhilarating experience, offering new sights, sounds, and experiences that enrich your life. However, for those of us with ADHD, the idea of traveling can sometimes feel as daunting as it is exciting. The key to successful travel lies in thorough preparation, adaptable strategies, and choosing the right destinations that match our unique needs and preferences.

Preparation Tips for Travel

Getting ready for a trip involves more than just packing a bag. It starts with meticulous planning, which can be a challenging task when your ADHD makes it tough to focus on details or foresee potential issues. Begin by outlining your itinerary with clear, simple steps. Use tools like travel apps or a physical planner to keep track of reservations, tickets, and important addresses. Packing can be made easier by using a checklist that you revise and reuse for each trip, ensuring you don't forget essentials like medication, chargers, or important documents.

Managing medications and routines while away from home is crucial. If you're traveling across time zones, adjust the times you take medications ahead of the trip to align with your destination's time zone. This can help mitigate the impact of jet lag and keep your medication's efficacy steady. Also, try to mimic at-home routines that help manage your ADHD. Whether it's morning meditation, reading before bed, or jotting down daily plans, maintaining these routines can provide a sense of stability amidst the chaos of travel.

Managing ADHD Symptoms While Traveling

Keeping your ADHD symptoms in check while traveling is pivotal. The unpredictability of travel can exacerbate symptoms, so maintaining some routine is beneficial. Use checklists daily to keep track of tasks such as confirming flight times, hotel check-in procedures, and planned activities. These not only aid in memory recall but also provide visual progress of your day, which can be incredibly satisfying.

Flexibility is also essential. No matter how well you plan, travel is fraught with unexpected changes. Instead of rigidly sticking to an itinerary, allow some leeway to adjust plans as needed. This reduces stress and makes it easier to cope with the unpredictable nature of travel. For instance, if a museum visit is taking longer than expected and you're enjoying it, it might be worth shifting other plans slightly to accommodate this unexpected joy.

Choosing ADHD-Friendly Destinations

When selecting a destination, consider what environments you thrive in. Do bustling cities energize you, or do they overwhelm you? Would a quiet countryside retreat suit you better? Think about the level of activity and the types of accommodations available. Destinations that offer a variety of structured activities, as well as opportunities for downtime, are usually a good choice. Look for accommodations that are comfortable and distraction-free. Hotels with business centers or quiet zones can be advantageous if you need to work or plan your days in a calm environment.

Dealing with Travel Anxiety

Travel anxiety is common, especially for those with ADHD, as the break from routine and the fear of unknowns can be triggering. To manage this anxiety, start by familiarizing yourself with travel details. Research your destination thoroughly, look at maps, read about the local culture, and understand what to expect from the weather. This knowledge can make the unknown more familiar and less daunting.

Mindfulness techniques can also be a great tool to manage anxiety. Engage in breathing exercises or guided meditations that you can do anywhere, anytime you start feeling overwhelmed. Having a supportive travel companion or group can also make a significant difference. They can not only share the burden of travel logistics but also provide emotional support, making the trip more enjoyable and less stressful.

Traveling with ADHD doesn't have to be an overwhelming challenge. With the right preparations, strategies for managing symptoms, careful choice of destinations, and techniques to handle anxiety, it can turn into a delightful adventure. These strategies not only make traveling smoother but also enrich your experiences, allowing you to enjoy the new and the unknown with confidence and joy.

Remember that each strategy, from diet and exercise to organizing your space and traveling, is about creating an environment that supports your needs and enhances your well-being. These changes, while sometimes small, can significantly improve your ability to manage ADHD and lead a fulfilling life. Next, we'll explore how leveraging technology can further aid in managing ADHD, providing tools and resources that make day-to-day living even smoother.

LEVERAGING TECHNOLOGY AND TOOLS

With ADHD, navigating through daily tasks can sometimes feel like trying to walk through a maze blindfolded. But what if I told you that the right digital tools could transform that maze into a well-lit path? In this chapter, we'll explore how technology can be tailored to meet the unique challenges of ADHD, turning potential obstacles into opportunities for streamlined productivity and enhanced daily living.

Apps and Digital Tools for Everyday ADHD Challenges

In the sea of apps available today, a few stand out for their utility in managing the every day challenges posed by ADHD. These apps act like lighthouses, guiding us through the fog of forgetfulness, distraction, and poor time management. From simple to-do lists to complex project management tools, the right app can make an enormous difference in how effectively we navigate our day.

I mentioned earlier the app **Todoist.** It's designed to manage tasks with features that allow you to set deadlines, prioritize tasks using color coding, and even delegate them to others. For someone with ADHD, the ability to visually categorize tasks by priority and see them checked off as completed can provide a tangible sense of accomplishment. Another invaluable tool is **Trello**. It uses cards and boards to organize projects, ideal for visual thinkers. You can create a card for each task and move it across the board as it progresses, from 'To Do' to 'Doing' to 'Done.' This visual progression can help maintain focus and motivation.

When looking for apps to aid with ADHD, several features are particularly beneficial. User-friendly interfaces are crucial—complex systems can become frustrating and are likely to be abandoned. Customizable notifications are another essential feature. For example, setting multiple reminders for a single task—like starting a project, a halfway check-in, and a pre-deadline alert—can help in maintaining focus and pacing your work. Additionally, the ability to sync across multiple devices ensures that you have access to your tasks and schedules, whether you're on your phone, tablet, or computer, making it easier to stay on top of your responsibilities no matter where you are.

Let's consider a case study to illustrate these points. Emily, a graphic designer with ADHD, struggled with meeting project deadlines and managing client expectations. By integrating Asana into her workflow, a tool known for its task management capabilities, she was able to break her projects into smaller, manageable tasks, each with its own deadline. The app's reminder system helped her stay on top of each phase of her projects, and the satisfaction of checking off completed tasks provided a motivational boost. This not only improved her productivity but also reduced her anxiety, as she could visually track her progress and anticipate the demands of upcoming tasks.

Assessing the effectiveness of an app in managing ADHD symptoms is crucial. Here are a few criteria to consider: Does the app adapt to your personal needs? Is it easy to use, or do you find yourself struggling to understand its features? Most importantly, does it make a noticeable difference in managing your symptoms—whether it's reducing forgetfulness, improving focus, or helping you manage time more effectively? An app that meets these criteria can be considered a valuable tool in your ADHD management toolkit.

By embracing these digital tools, you can create a supportive framework that complements your efforts to manage ADHD. These apps don't just help organize your tasks; they enhance your ability to function effectively in your personal and professional life, turning the chaos of ADHD into a structured dance. With each notification, each checked-off task, and each synchronized schedule, you're not just using an app; you're mastering your interactions with the world around you, one tap at a time.

Customizing Technology to Enhance Personal Productivity

When it comes to the digital environment, think of it as your personal workspace—not just physically but mentally as well. Having tools and settings that align with your ADHD can change the game by minimizing distractions and enhancing your productivity. The magic lies in customization, making your devices work for you in a way that complements how your mind operates. Let's explore how you can turn your everyday gadgets into allies, fine-tuned to help manage your ADHD symptoms.

Starting with personalization of your devices, it's like setting up a living space that feels like home. Your smartphone, tablet, and computer can be transformed into environments that promote focus and efficiency. Begin by **tailoring notifications.** Notifications can be a major distraction, constantly pulling your attention away from the task at hand. Customize these alerts by deciding which apps can send you notifications and at what times. Most devices allow you to schedule 'Do Not Disturb' modes during which only priority contacts can reach you. This can be particularly useful during work hours or while you're dedicated to deep-focus tasks. Next, organize your apps and files. A cluttered digital desktop can be as chaotic as a messy physical workspace. Group related apps into folders, keep frequently used apps on your home screen and archive old files and apps you no longer use. This reduces visual clutter and makes navigation smoother and faster, aligning with the quick pace at which your ADHD brain works.

Automation tools provide another layer of support, handling routine tasks that might slip through the cracks of a distracted mind. Tools like IFTTT (If This Then That) or Zapier are fantastic for setting up automated actions that help streamline your day. For example, you can create an automation where an email from your boss automatically gets flagged and added to your to-do list. Or, set up a routine that turns off smart home lights and electronics at a certain time, helping you wind down before bed without needing to remember every single switch. These tools do more than just save time; they reduce the cognitive load, freeing up your mental space for more important or enjoyable tasks.

Productivity software often comes packed with features, but a few are particularly beneficial for ADHD. Microsoft Office and Google Suite, for instance, offer **focus modes and voice-to-text options.** Focus mode in Microsoft Word dims everything except the paragraph you are working on, minimizing visual distractions. Voice-to-text can be incredibly useful if you find it easier to speak your thoughts than to type them. This feature captures your words as text in real time, which can help with capturing fleeting ideas before they escape your attention. Utilizing these features can transform your approach to tasks, allowing you to work with your ADHD rather than against it.

Finally, setting up productive workspaces on your digital devices is key. If you work primarily on a computer, consider using multiple monitors. This setup can help you keep reference material on one screen and your work document on another, reducing the need to switch back and forth between tabs, a common distraction trigger. Additionally, consider using website blockers during work hours to prevent the temptation of browsing non-work-related sites. Software like **Cold Turkey or**

Freedom can block distracting websites, apps, and even the entire internet for set periods, helping you stay focused on the task at part.

By customizing your technology in these ways, you create a digital environment that supports your unique working style and ADHD needs. This isn't just about being more productive; it's about feeling more in control and less overwhelmed by your tasks. Your devices become tools of empowerment, tailored to help you navigate your day with greater ease and confidence. Whether it's through tailored notifications, automated routines, specialized software features, or optimized workspaces, the right technological setup can make a substantial difference in managing your ADHD and enhancing your daily productivity.

Technology Tips:

- Project management apps: Todoist and Trello, can help with deadlines and daily tasks

- Tailoring notifications – create a space that is less distracting, you don't need every alert on

- Focus modes and voice-to-text options: minimize visual distractions and capture fleeting ideas

- Website blockers: install software like Cold Turkey or Freedom to block distracting websites and apps for set periods of time

Online Communities and Support: Navigating the Digital Space

Finding the right community, especially when you're trying to navigate the complexities of ADHD, can sometimes feel like searching for a quiet corner in a bustling cafe. It's about finding a spot where the noise dims, and you can hear your own thoughts while feeling the support of those around you. In the digital age, online communities provide this space for many of us, offering a sanctuary where questions can be asked, experiences shared, and understanding fostered without ever leaving our homes. Whether it's through social media platforms, dedicated forums, or apps designed specifically for mental health support, these communities are invaluable.

When you start looking for the right online ADHD community, think about what you hope to find. Are you looking for advice on managing daily tasks or perhaps a space to vent and receive support from those who really understand? Maybe you're seeking the latest research or discussions about medication and therapies. Platforms like **Reddit and Facebook** offer a variety of ADHD-specific groups, each with its own focus and atmosphere. For a more interactive experience, forums on websites like **ADDitude Magazine** provide a platform for deeper discussions and even access to experts during scheduled events. Apps designed for mental health support, such as **Wisdo or HealthUnlocked,** can also connect you to a broader community of individuals facing similar challenges, offering structured support and resources.

The benefits of engaging with these communities are manifold. First, there's the accessibility. No matter where you are or what time it is, you can log in and find someone to talk to or scroll through past discussions that might address your current concerns. This 24/7 availability can be a lifeline during moments of frustration or isolation. Anonymity is another significant advantage. If you're not comfortable with sharing your struggles with ADHD openly, online platforms can offer a space to speak freely without fear of judgment, allowing for honesty and openness that might be harder to achieve face-to-face. Furthermore, the diversity of perspectives in these communities can be incredibly enriching. You'll find people from all walks of life, each managing their ADHD in different ways, providing a wealth of strategies and insights that you might not encounter in your day-to-day life.

However, navigating online interactions does require some care. It's important to manage your personal information wisely. Be cautious about what personal details you share, even in private messages, as online platforms can be vulnerable to security breaches. Also, be aware of the community's guidelines and the general etiquette to ensure positive interactions. Unfortunately, online spaces can sometimes harbor trolls or negative interactions. If you encounter this, most platforms allow you to report inappropriate content or block users who are detracting from your experience rather than enhancing it. Remember, the goal of joining these communities is to support your journey with ADHD, not to add to your stress.

Leveraging online resources to learn about ADHD management can further enhance your experience in these communities. Many platforms offer free webinars, interactive courses, and podcasts tailored to ADHD challenges. For instance, ADDitude Magazine frequently hosts webinars with experts on various aspects of ADHD, from medication management to organization skills and emotional regulation. YouTube channels, like How to ADHD, provide insightful tips and strategies in an engaging format. Engaging with these resources can not only deepen your understanding of ADHD but also equip you with practical tools to manage your symptoms more effectively.

By thoughtfully engaging with online communities and resources, you can significantly enrich your management of ADHD. These digital spaces offer not just information and strategies but also a sense of belonging and understanding—a community that sees and supports you, where being different doesn't mean being alone. As you continue to explore and interact in these spaces, remember that every shared story and every piece of advice enriches not only your own experience but also that of others, creating a vibrant tapestry of shared wisdom and support.

Privacy and ADHD: Managing Digital Footprints

Navigating the digital world with ADHD can sometimes feel like trying to keep track of a hundred tennis balls lobbed at you all at once. Your focus might dart from one alert to the next, passwords might slip through the cracks of your memory, and before you know it, your digital presence feels as scattered as your thoughts on a hectic day. Understanding digital privacy and managing your online footprint is crucial, not just to protect yourself from external threats but also to keep your digital life manageable and orderly.

Let's talk about why digital privacy matters, especially for you. With ADHD, the impulse to click, share, or explore online can sometimes lead you down risky paths. The internet is a labyrinth of information and interaction, where personal details are too easily dispersed and where distractions abound. Each shared detail, each saved password, and every app permission you grant can increase your vulnerability to data breaches, identity theft, and other digital dangers. Plus, the scattered nature of ADHD might make it harder to keep track of what information you've shared and where making you more susceptible to privacy risks.

Best practices for maintaining online privacy start with the basics—**strong, unique passwords for each site or service.** A password manager can be a lifesaver here, storing your passwords securely and automatically filling them in when needed, so you don't have to rely on your memory or use easily guessable passwords. Next, consider the security of your internet connections. Using VPNs (Virtual Private Networks) can encrypt your internet traffic, hiding your online activities from prying eyes and protecting your data from hackers, especially when you're on public Wi-Fi. Secure browsers and private browsing modes can also prevent tracking cookies from logging your online behavior, adding an extra layer of privacy.

Now, on to managing digital clutter, which is an often overlooked aspect of digital privacy. Just like physical clutter can overwhelm your senses and make it hard to focus, digital clutter can lead to information overload and increased anxiety, not to mention greater risks to your privacy. Regular digital clean-ups are essential. This means unsubscribing from unneeded email lists, deleting old accounts, and clearing out redundant files. These actions reduce the 'noise' in your digital life and minimize the points where your information is stored, thereby decreasing the chances of your data being compromised.

Let's explore some tools that can enhance your privacy protection.

Tools like privacy-focused web browsers, such as **Brave or Firefox Focus,** automatically block trackers and ads that can compromise your privacy. They also offer various privacy protections right out of the box, requiring minimal customization. For managing app permissions on your smartphone, tools like **Bouncer for Android** allow you to grant permissions temporarily. This means an app can access your camera or location only when it's actively being used and not in the background, keeping you in control of your data.

By taking these steps towards securing your digital presence, you create a safer and more streamlined online experience that aligns with your needs and lifestyle. Protecting your digital privacy isn't just about security; it's about constructing a digital environment that supports your focus and productivity, reducing stress, and enhancing your ability to manage your ADHD effectively. As you continue to apply these practices, remember that each small adjustment contributes to a larger picture of safety and efficiency, helping you navigate the digital world with greater confidence and peace of mind.

Gadgets That Simplify Life for the ADHD Brain

Let's dive into the world of wearable technology, which has opened a new frontier for managing ADHD. Imagine a gadget that sits quietly on your wrist, not only telling the time but also nudging you gently with reminders throughout your day. This isn't science fiction—it's the reality offered by smartwatches and fitness trackers. These devices have become invaluable for many with ADHD by serving as external memory aids. They can remind you of appointments, when to take medication, or even prompt you to start winding down for bed, integrating seamlessly into daily life to provide the right nudges at the right time. For instance, many smartwatches offer features like setting multiple alarms that can be labeled for specific tasks and vibrating gently to catch your attention without overwhelming you. Some even offer sleep tracking, which can be particularly useful if you're trying to understand your sleep patterns and how they affect your ADHD symptoms. By monitoring your sleep, you can make informed adjustments to improve both your rest and your focus during the day.

Transitioning into the realm of home life, smart home devices offer another layer of support that can be transformative. **Voice-activated assistants** can act as your personal secretary, setting reminder timers and even helping with task lists without requiring you to tap on a screen or press a button. Imagine cooking dinner and remembering you need to send an important email. Instead of dropping everything to find your phone or laptop, you could simply speak the reminder out loud, and your assistant would take care of setting it up. **Smart lighting** can also play a subtle yet effective role in managing your ADHD. Lights that adjust the color temperature with the time of day can help regulate your natural sleep-wake cycle, promoting better sleep and more alert mornings. **Automated appliances** can handle tasks that often slip your mind, like turning off the oven or adjusting the thermostat, reducing daily stress and potential safety concerns.

Now, let's explore some specialized gadgets designed with ADHD needs in mind. **Noise-canceling headphones** are a game-changer for many with ADHD, especially those with sensory processing sensitivities. In environments like open offices or busy cafes, background noise can scatter your thoughts and pull your focus in a thousand directions. By wearing noise-canceling headphones, you can create a bubble of calm around you, allowing you to focus deeply, whether you're working, studying, or simply trying to unwind. Another intriguing development in ADHD-specific gadgets is the rise of fidget tools—devices designed to engage your hands quietly while allowing your mind to remain focused on the task at hand. Unlike the often-distracting fidget spinners that became a craze, these tools are subtler and designed to be used without drawing much attention, perfect for maintaining focus during meetings or while working at your desk.

Evaluating the effectiveness of these gadgets is crucial to ensure they are more than just novel distractions. When considering a new gadget, think about what specific challenges you want it to address. Is it forgetfulness, sensory overload, or perhaps time management? Then, look at features that directly mitigate these challenges. Cost is also an essential factor; it's important to weigh the initial investment against the potential benefits. How much time and stress could this gadget save you? Read reviews from other users with ADHD to get a sense of how the gadget works in day-to-day scenarios. Personal adaptability is another critical criterion. A gadget should fit seamlessly into your lifestyle and be intuitive enough not to require constant troubleshooting or adjustments. It's about finding tools that integrate effortlessly into your life, enhancing your ability to manage your symptoms without adding complexity.

By incorporating these gadgets into your daily routine, you can leverage technology to address specific ADHD challenges, creating an environment that supports your needs and allows you to focus more on what truly matters. Whether it's through wearable tech that keeps you on track, smart home devices that simplify daily tasks, or specialized gadgets that help maintain focus, the right tools can make all the difference in managing ADHD effectively and living a more organized, less stressful life.

Using Social Media Wisely with ADHD

Navigating social media with ADHD can sometimes feel like you're a kid turned loose in a candy store—everything is tempting, colorful, and just a click away. However, just as too much candy can lead to a stomachache, too much social media can lead to an overload of information, distraction, and even anxiety. For those of us with ADHD, the dynamic and ever-changing nature of social media feeds can hook our attention a bit too effectively, leading to hours lost in a digital haze. This hyperfocus on scrolling through updates can eat into time meant for other tasks, disrupt sleep patterns, and even impact our emotional well-being due to the constant barrage of information and social comparison.

But it's not all doom and gloom. Social media, when used strategically, can be a powerful ally. It's about setting boundaries and using tools that help manage how and when you engage with social media platforms. One effective strategy is setting specific time limits for social media use. Most smartphones now offer features that allow you to monitor your screen time and set limits for specific apps. By allocating a set amount of time per day for social media, you can enjoy staying connected without it overtaking your life. Additionally, consider customizing your notifications. Turning off non-essential alerts can significantly reduce distractions, helping you regain control over your attention and reduce the impulse to check your phone every few minutes.

Moreover, curating your social media feeds can transform your experience from one of distraction to one of enrichment. Unfollow accounts or mute posts that trigger anxiety or lead you to mindlessly scroll, and instead, follow pages that inspire and uplift you or provide useful information. This selective approach helps in creating a digital environment that supports your well-being and keeps you engaged in a positive way. It's like tidying up your digital room, where you keep only what brings joy or value, making your time spent on social media more satisfying and less overwhelming.

Social media also opens up wonderful opportunities for networking and advocacy, particularly for the ADHD community. Platforms like Twitter, Facebook, and LinkedIn can be invaluable for connecting with others who share similar challenges and experiences. These connections can lead to opportunities for collaboration, finding support, and exchanging tips on managing ADHD. Moreover, social media can be a powerful platform for advocacy, raising awareness about ADHD, and challenging the stigma that often surrounds mental health issues. By sharing your own stories and supporting ADHD advocacy groups online, you can contribute to a greater understanding and acceptance of ADHD, helping to foster a more inclusive and supportive community.

Balancing our online and offline lives is crucial, especially when our brains are wired to seek out constant stimulation. It's important to create clear distinctions between time spent engaging online and time spent in the physical world. Regularly unplugging from digital devices and engaging in activities that ground you in the real world—like spending time in nature, practicing mindfulness, or enjoying hobbies—can help maintain this balance. These activities not only provide a necessary break from digital stimulation but also enhance your overall well-being, keeping your mind sharp and your spirit calm.

Embracing these strategies can significantly improve how you interact with social media, turning it from a potential source of distraction into a tool that supports your personal and professional life. By setting boundaries, curating your feed, leveraging social media for networking and advocacy, and balancing your online and offline activities, you can harness the benefits of these platforms while managing their challenges effectively.

We've uncovered various ways to tailor digital resources to better suit our unique needs as individuals with ADHD. From customizing apps and devices to enhance productivity to navigating social media wisely, each strategy offers a pathway to more efficient and effective management of your daily life. These tools are not just about staying organized or meeting deadlines; they are about creating a lifestyle that allows you to thrive with ADHD. As we transition into the next chapter, we'll delve deeper into personal development strategies that build on these technological tools, helping you to further refine your skills and embrace your strengths in a world that never stops moving.

MINDSET AND EMOTIONAL HEALTH: BUILDING A POSITIVE ADHD IDENTITY

Picture yourself in a bustling orchestra, where each instrument plays its own tune, creating a cacophony of sounds. Now imagine trying to focus on a single melody amidst this symphony, with your mind amplifying every note, rhythm, and emotion. This is a glimpse into the daily experiences of someone living with ADHD. The constant barrage can be overwhelming, often painting ADHD as a deficit in the narrative of one's life. But what if we shift that narrative? What if we view this heightened perception not as a deficit but as a different way of experiencing the world, rich with potential for creativity and depth?

Reframing ADHD: From Deficit to Difference

Changing the Narrative: When you hear the term "ADHD," it's often flanked by negatives—"disorder," "deficit," or "dysfunction." These words carry weight; they shape how we see ourselves and how others see us. But let's step back for a moment and reconsider this perspective. ADHD does involve challenges, but it also brings with it a unique set of cognitive patterns and abilities. Imagine a world where these traits are not just accepted but valued. A world where the rapid-fire connections made by your brain are seen as a source of creativity, where your ability to hyper-focus gives you an edge in problem-solving. This isn't just wishful thinking—it's about shifting the focus from what we struggle with to what we excel in. By changing the narrative from a deficit-focused view to one that recognizes ADHD as a different way of thinking, we empower ourselves to redefine our experiences and our identities.

Scientific Insights: The concept of neurodiversity supports this reframed understanding of ADHD. Neurodiversity is a perspective that brain differences are normal and that neurological variations such as ADHD are simply variations in human cognition, not defects. This view is supported by numerous studies in psychology and neuroscience that highlight the adaptive qualities of various neurodivergent traits. For instance, while the ADHD brain may struggle with traditional organizational tasks, it is often better at processing information in a high-stimulus environment, a trait that can be advantageous in fields such as emergency services, creative arts, or entrepreneurship. These insights challenge the traditional pathology-oriented view of ADHD and open up a dialogue about the diverse ways in which the human brain can excel.

Real-Life Examples: Consider the stories of well-known individuals who have turned their ADHD traits into assets. Richard Branson, founder of the Virgin Group, credits his success in the chaotic world of entrepreneurship to his ADHD traits, stating that his ability to maintain enthusiasm and think outside the box are direct results of his ADHD. Similarly, Simone Biles, a celebrated gymnast, has spoken about how her hyperfocus, a trait common in those with ADHD, has been a crucial element in her training regimen and competitive performances. These examples serve not just as inspiration but as concrete evidence of how

ADHD traits can be leveraged to achieve extraordinary success.

Impact on Self-Esteem: Understanding ADHD through the lens of difference rather than deficit can have a profound impact on self-esteem. For many, being diagnosed with ADHD comes with a baggage of perceived failures—struggles in school, difficulties at work, and challenges in personal relationships. However, by reframing ADHD, we start to see these experiences not as failures but as signs of a need for different strategies and environments. This shift in perspective can reduce feelings of inadequacy and help build a more positive self-image. It encourages a kinder self-dialogue, one that acknowledges challenges but also celebrates unique strengths and successes.

By redefining ADHD in terms of difference rather than deficit, we open up a new realm of possibilities for personal growth and achievement. This shift not only enhances our understanding of ourselves but also enriches the ways in which we connect with the world. As we continue to explore and embrace the unique facets of ADHD, we pave the way for a more inclusive and appreciative understanding of all minds.

Celebrating ADHD Strengths in Personal and Professional Life

When you think about your ADHD, what's the first thing that comes to mind? If you're like many, you might first focus on the difficulties—maybe it's the challenge of keeping track of time or staying organized. But what if, just for today, we shift our focus and spotlight the incredible strengths that often accompany ADHD? It's like turning a kaleidoscope; the same pieces that seemed scattered at one angle fall into a beautiful pattern at another. This new perspective isn't just about feeling good; it's about recognizing and leveraging the unique abilities that ADHD brings into your life.

Identifying Personal Strengths: Let's start by identifying these strengths. Many individuals with ADHD exhibit remarkable resilience—the ability to bounce back from setbacks and keep going even in the face of difficulties. This resilience often develops through years of navigating the ups and downs of ADHD. Then there's creativity; the ADHD brain is a powerhouse of new ideas, making connections that others might not see. And, of course, the ability to hyper-focus; when engaged in a task that truly interests you, the world fades away, allowing for deep and intense periods of productivity. To start seeing these traits in yourself, consider keeping a daily journal where you note moments you felt resilient, creative, or particularly focused. Over time, you'll begin to see patterns that highlight your unique strengths.

Leveraging Strengths at Work: In the workplace, these traits can be your greatest assets. Take creativity. In jobs that value innovation—marketing, design, entrepreneurship, or any role requiring problem-solving—your ability to think outside the box can make you a valuable team member. Start by embracing tasks that require brainstorming or creative thinking. Speak up in meetings, share your ideas, and don't be afraid to suggest unconventional approaches to projects. For hyper-focus, use it to your advantage during tasks that require intense concentration. Block out distractions and give yourself a set time to dive deep. This can be especially effective when working on complex problems or projects that require detailed attention. And resilience? It's all about mindset. View each challenge as an opportunity to learn and grow, and don't be shy about sharing your experiences with colleagues. Your ability to navigate challenges might just inspire others.

Enhancing Social Relationships: The same traits that make you unique can also enrich your personal relationships. The spontaneity and energy of ADHD can bring a dynamic and exciting element to your interactions with others. Your natural inclination towards creative thinking can make you a fun, engaging companion, always ready with a new idea for an adventure. Moreover, the resilience you've developed can help you handle the ups and downs of relationships with grace and perseverance. To deepen these connections, be open about your ADHD. Sharing your experiences can not only increase understanding but also create a deeper bond as you let others see and appreciate your world.

Role Models and Mentors: Navigating ADHD isn't a solo journey.

Across the globe, countless individuals have turned their ADHD traits into pathways for success, and many of them are eager to mentor others. Look for role models in the ADHD community—people who have harnessed their ADHD traits in ways that inspire you. This might be someone you meet in an online forum, a local support group, or even a public figure whose story resonates with you. Reach out to them, ask about their strategies for success, and learn from their experiences. Mentors can provide not just guidance but also encouragement, reminding you that your goals are achievable and that your ADHD traits are not just challenges to be managed but strengths to be celebrated.

Embracing and celebrating your ADHD strengths can transform how you see yourself and how you interact with the world. It's about more than just coping with symptoms; it's about thriving by recognizing the unique advantages your ADHD brings. Whether you're leveraging your creativity at work, enjoying deeper personal relationships, or learning from mentors who inspire you, remember that your ADHD is not just a list of challenges—it's a collection of potential strengths waiting to be realized.

Continuous Learning and ADHD: Strategies for Lifelong Growth

Learning isn't just about absorbing information; it's about adapting and growing continuously, making sense of the world in ways that enrich our lives and careers. For those of us with ADHD, the traditional methods of learning can sometimes feel like wearing clothes that just don't fit right—restrictive and uncomfortable. Recognizing this, it becomes essential to tailor our learning experiences to suit our unique way of processing information. Visual aids, hands-on experiences, and technology-based tools are not just accessories; they are necessities that can transform our learning journey into something that feels not only manageable but also enjoyable.

Think about the last time you tried to learn something new. Was it through a lengthy lecture or a thick manual? How much did you actually retain? Now, imagine learning the same concept through a video tutorial or by engaging in a hands-on project. Chances are, these methods would be more effective. Visual aids like infographics or diagrams help in breaking down complex information into digestible pieces, making it easier to understand and retain. Hands-on experiences, such as building a model or conducting an experiment, allow for experiential learning, which can be particularly beneficial for those of us with ADHD. It engages multiple senses and makes the learning process active rather than passive. Moreover, technology-based tools like educational apps or online platforms offer interactive and customizable learning experiences that can be paced according to individual needs.

Embracing a growth mindset is another cornerstone of effective learning, especially for adults with ADHD. The concept, popularized by psychologist Carol Dweck, suggests that our abilities and intelligence can be developed with time and effort. This mindset is particularly empowering for those of us with ADHD, as it shifts our focus from perceived limitations to potential growth. It encourages us to view challenges as opportunities to learn and develop rather than as insurmountable obstacles. This perspective can be liberating, especially after years of struggling with traditional learning environments that might not have recognized or accommodated our unique needs. By adopting a growth mindset, we open ourselves up to a world of possibilities where each mistake is a step forward, not a reason to give up.

In terms of resources, the digital age has provided us with an abundance of tools tailored to diverse learning needs. Online platforms like Coursera, Khan Academy, and LinkedIn Learning offer courses on a wide range of topics, many of which are designed with interactive elements to cater to different learning styles. These platforms often provide flexibility in terms of pacing and scheduling, which is ideal for adults with ADHD who might find strict schedules challenging. Additionally, books such as "Driven to Distraction" by Edward Hallowell and John Ratey offer insights into managing ADHD, including strategies for effective learning. Workshops and seminars that focus on skills development, such as time management or creative thinking, can also be invaluable, providing practical, hands-on learning experiences that can be directly applied to personal and professional life.

Feedback and self-assessment are crucial in this process, serving as compasses that guide our learning journey. Regular feedback, whether from peers, mentors, or through self-reflection, provides insights into our progress and areas that need adjustment. For someone with ADHD, structured feedback can help maintain focus on specific goals and can motivate continued effort and adjustment. Self-assessment is equally important; it involves stepping back regularly to review our own progress, celebrate our successes, and identify areas where we can improve. This could be as simple as keeping a learning journal where you reflect on what you've learned each week, what methods worked best, and what you found challenging. This ongoing process of feedback and self-assessment not only reinforces learning but also enhances self-awareness and self-esteem, empowering us to take charge of our educational paths and personal growth.

In embracing these strategies, we not only adapt learning to fit our ADHD but also turn it into a tool for personal and professional empowerment. By customizing how we learn, adopting a mindset that welcomes growth, utilizing diverse resources, and engaging in regular feedback and self-assessment, we transform learning from a chore into an ongoing adventure that continually enriches our lives. As we integrate these practices, learning becomes less about reaching a specific endpoint and more about evolving continuously, adapting not just to survive but to thrive.

Creativity and Innovation: Harnessing ADHD Superpowers

Imagine if you could see your ADHD not just as a series of hurdles but as a treasure trove of untapped creative potential. It's a bit like finding out that the quirky old lamp you've had for years is actually a magic lantern. The secret to unlocking this magic? Understanding how ADHD often correlates with a high capacity for creativity and divergent thinking. Research in cognitive neuroscience suggests that the ADHD brain exhibits increased neural activity in areas responsible for creative thinking and problem-solving. This heightened activity can lead to an ability to generate a vast array of ideas, see unique connections between concepts, and find original solutions to problems. Essentially, while the ADHD brain may struggle with linear tasks and routines, it thrives in environments that demand innovative and out-of-the-box thinking.

To tap into this creative potential, integrating daily creative practices into your routine can be transformative. Think of creativity as a muscle—the more you exercise it, the stronger it becomes. Simple practices like keeping a creativity journal can be a great start. Every day, spend a few minutes jotting down any new ideas you have, no matter how outlandish they may seem. Sketch, doodle, or write—it doesn't matter the medium as long as you're allowing your mind the freedom to roam. You might also try 'creative sprints' where, for 10-15 minutes, you challenge yourself to come up with as many solutions as possible to a fun problem. These exercises can help condition your mind to continue producing creative thoughts, effectively turning everyday inspiration into innovative ideas.

Bringing creativity into the workplace can sometimes feel like trying to plant a garden in a desert. The professional environment doesn't always make room for the kind of radical thinking and risk-taking that true innovation requires. However, with your natural ADHD-driven creativity, you are uniquely equipped to introduce and promote innovative ideas. Start by identifying opportunities where new approaches are needed and propose solutions that might not have been considered. When presenting these ideas, frame them in a way that aligns with your organization's goals and show how they can lead to improved outcomes. This not only places your ideas in a constructive light but also positions you as a forward-thinker capable of steering the company toward future successes.

Celebrating your creative successes plays a crucial role in reinforcing your identity as an innovator. Whether it's a new process that improves efficiency at work or a personal project that you've seen to fruition, take the time to acknowledge and celebrate these achievements. This could be as simple as sharing your accomplishments with friends or colleagues or as much as posting about your project on social media. You might even consider creating a 'success portfolio,' a collection of projects and feedback that you can look back on to remind yourself of your creative capabilities. This portfolio can also be a valuable tool in professional settings, providing concrete examples of your ability to think differently and produce results.

By embracing the link between ADHD and creativity, integrating daily practices that enhance your innovative thinking, effectively introducing new ideas in the workplace, and taking the time to celebrate your creative achievements, you harness the true potential of your ADHD superpowers. This approach not only enriches your personal and professional life but also shifts your narrative from one of struggling with ADHD to one of thriving because of it. It's about flipping the script, seeing the strengths in your struggles, and realizing that within you lies a wellspring of creativity waiting to be unleashed.

> **ADHD thought:**
>
> What is your ADHD superpower? Where have you had wild ideas but didn't explore the possibilities? Write them down and collect them and never stop dreaming.

Advocating for Yourself: ADHD in the Workplace and Beyond

Navigating the professional world with ADHD can sometimes feel like you're playing a complex game without fully understanding the rules. This is where self-advocacy becomes not just helpful but essential. It's about more than just speaking up; it's about understanding your needs, communicating them effectively, and crafting an environment where you can thrive. Think of self-advocacy as your voice in the chorus of the workplace, ensuring that it harmonizes with the others while still being distinctly heard.

Self-advocacy starts with a clear communication of your needs. It's important to articulate what accommodations or adjustments would help you perform at your best. This could mean asking for a quiet space to work to reduce sensory overload or perhaps requesting written instructions instead of verbal ones to better process information. When approaching these conversations, it's crucial to frame your requests in a way that emphasizes the mutual benefits: explain how these accommodations will not only support your productivity but also enhance your contributions to the team. Remember, effective self-advocacy is rooted in a deep understanding of your own ADHD-related challenges and strengths. It requires a thoughtful assessment of how your environment impacts your performance and what specific changes could help mitigate challenges.

Understanding your legal rights is another vital component of self-advocacy. In many countries, ADHD is recognized under disability rights laws, which can provide protection against discrimination and a legal framework for requesting reasonable accommodations at work. Familiarizing yourself with these rights can empower you to advocate for yourself with confidence. It's about knowing the safety nets that are in place to support you and how to effectively leverage them if needed. For instance, in the United States, the **Americans with Disabilities Act (ADA)** requires employers to provide reasonable accommodations to qualified employees with disabilities, including those with ADHD, provided they do not impose undue hardship on the operation of the business. Understanding these protections not only arms you with knowledge but also with a sense of security, knowing that there are laws that recognize and support your needs.

Building a support network within your workplace is equally crucial. This network can include understanding colleagues, empathetic supervisors, or even a human resources (HR) department that is knowledgeable about ADHD and inclusive practices. Start by identifying allies who show a willingness to understand or share your approach to work. These connections can provide not just emotional support but can also advocate alongside you when needed. Participating in or even establishing support groups or networks for employees with ADHD or other neurodivergent conditions can further strengthen your support system. These groups can offer a platform for sharing strategies, experiences, and resources, enhancing your sense of community and belonging at work.

Lastly, enhancing your public speaking and presentation skills can significantly boost your self-advocacy efforts. For many with ADHD, the dynamic nature of public speaking can actually be a strength. Your passion and ability to think divergently can be captivating in a speaking scenario. To hone these skills, consider joining a workshop or a group like Toastmasters, which can provide a supportive environment to practice and receive feedback. Focus on structuring your presentations to play to your strengths, such as using visual aids or interactive elements to keep your audience engaged. Additionally, practice techniques to manage common ADHD symptoms that might interfere, such as distractibility or time management during your talk. By developing strong speaking skills, you not only enhance your ability to advocate for yourself but also boost your overall confidence in professional settings.

Self-advocacy is a powerful tool in navigating the complexities of the workplace with ADHD. It involves clear communication, a solid understanding of your rights, building supportive networks, and enhancing your public engagement skills. Each element plays a crucial role in not just surviving but thriving in your career. As you continue to develop these skills, you'll find that advocating for yourself becomes less daunting and more of a natural part of your professional journey, one that empowers you to shape your work environment to better suit your unique needs and talents.

Building a Legacy: Long-Term Goal Setting with ADHD

Imagine you're embarking on a road trip without a map, guided only by the desire to explore. While spontaneous journeys can bring unexpected joys, they can also lead to chaotic meanderings. For those with ADHD, the path to achieving long-term goals can sometimes feel like this—a journey without a clear map. However, by developing a vision for your future and setting structured goals aligned with your passions and strengths, you create a roadmap that not only directs your energies but also maximizes your unique ADHD attributes.

When you start to envision your future, think about what truly excites you—those activities that ignite your passion and engage your full attention. Whether it's a career ambition, a personal development goal, or a creative endeavor, defining these aspirations is the first step toward creating a fulfilling legacy. Use visualization techniques to make these goals vivid: imagine where you want to be in five years, the achievements you wish to celebrate, or the impacts you hope to have. This mental imagery serves not just as motivation but also as a guide to defining clearer, actionable objectives.

Strategic planning is crucial, especially for those with ADHD who might struggle with staying on course. Traditional methods of planning often emphasize rigid structures and timelines, which can be stifling. Instead, consider flexible planning techniques that allow for adjustments as needed, catering to the dynamic nature of ADHD. For instance, instead of setting daily tasks that might become overwhelming, you could outline broader weekly goals that give you the flexibility to manage how and when you meet them based on your fluctuating focus and energy levels. Tools like digital calendars or planning apps can be instrumental here, enabling you to set reminders for deadlines and automate repetitive tasks, which helps conserve mental energy for more critical decision-making.

Monitoring your progress is another key element in the journey towards your goals. It can be easy to lose sight of achievements, especially when they are incremental. Utilizing tools like progress-tracking apps or maintaining a goal journal can provide you with concrete evidence of your advancements. These tools allow you to set milestones and review your progress regularly, adjusting your strategies as necessary. This ongoing assessment helps maintain your motivation, a crucial factor in ADHD management, where interest can wane if results aren't immediately apparent. Moreover, sharing your progress with a mentor or a peer group can offer you valuable feedback and the added benefit of accountability.

Celebrating milestones is essential. Each goal reached or milestone achieved is a testament to your perseverance and skill. Make it a point to acknowledge these successes, no matter how small. This could be as simple as a small treat for yourself or a social gathering to share your achievements with friends and family. These celebrations reinforce positive behaviors and remind you that your efforts are yielding results, boosting your confidence and enthusiasm to pursue further goals. It's about creating positive reinforcement loops that continually remind you of your capabilities and successes, fostering a sustained effort toward building your personal legacy.

In wrapping up this chapter, we've explored the transformative power of setting and achieving long-term goals through a lens tailored for ADHD. From crafting a vivid vision to leveraging flexible planning techniques, monitoring progress, and celebrating each success, these strategies are designed to guide you in forging a path that honors your unique strengths and challenges. As you apply these insights, you're not just working toward external achievements; you're also building a deeper understanding and appreciation of your journey with ADHD.

Your ADHD narrative:

- In what ways have you thought ADHD as a limitation? What thought can you replace that with?

- What would you like to achieve in the following year? Where do you need help with this?

- What kind of legacy do you want to leave?

CONCLUSION

As we draw the curtains on this journey together, I want to take a moment to reflect on the path we've navigated, transforming the challenges of ADHD into remarkable strengths. We began with a view of ADHD often seen through a lens of deficit, but together, we shifted our perspective to recognize it as a unique constellation of cognitive patterns, brimming with potential for creativity and unparalleled problem-solving capabilities.

Understanding and managing executive functions has emerged as a cornerstone of our discussions, vital for success in both your personal and professional spheres. These skills are not just tools; they are bridges connecting you to your goals, aspirations, and dreams. We delved into five key strategies that I hope have illuminated your path—Strategic Time Management, Enhancing Focus and Productivity, Emotional Intelligence and Resilience, Building and Maintaining Relationships, and Lifestyle Adjustments for ADHD Management. Each strategy, a stepping stone, is designed to guide you toward a more balanced and fulfilling life.

We also explored the powerful role of technology and tools in supporting your daily management of ADHD symptoms. These innovations are not just conveniences; they are lifelines that enhance productivity and bring balance to the bustling chaos that can sometimes define our lives with ADHD.

Reflecting on your personal growth journey, we've seen how developing a positive ADHD identity is deeply transformative. Embracing continuous learning, unleashing your innate creativity, advocating for yourself, and setting long-term goals are not just chapters in a book but chapters in your life, each adding depth and richness to your story.

Embrace your ADHD. Utilize the strategies, tools, and insights we've shared to navigate your challenges and harness your strengths. View your ADHD not as an obstacle but as a vibrant opportunity for growth, innovation, and success. Start applying these strategies in your daily life, and let each step forward be a testament to your resilience and creativity.

Remember, the journey of personal development is continuous. Approaching it with patience, self-compassion, and persistence is crucial. Mastering executive functioning skills and building a fulfilling life with ADHD is an evolving process, one that requires time, effort, and heart.

I also invite you to connect with the broader ADHD community. There is immense power in shared experiences and collective wisdom. Online resources, support groups, and advocacy organizations can provide not just support and inspiration but also a platform for empowerment and advocacy.

In closing, I extend to you my deepest gratitude for joining me on this enlightening journey. My hope and confidence in your ability to transform your ADHD challenges into avenues for personal and professional success are boundless. Thank you for allowing me to be a part of your story, for sharing your challenges and triumphs, and for striving every day to see beyond the horizon.

Together, let's continue to redefine ADHD, turning every struggle into a stride toward triumph. Here's to your journey, your victories, and the incredible potential of your unique and brilliant mind.

REFERENCES

- Additude. (n.d.). *The ADHD brain: Neuroscience behind attention deficit.* Retrieved from https://www.additudemag.com/adhd-neuroscience-101/#:~:text=ADHD%20seems%20to%20involve%20impaired,%2C%20organization%2C%20and%20executive%20function.

- Additude. (n.d.). *Time management skills for ADHD brains: Practical advice.* Retrieved from https://www.additudemag.com/time-management-skills-adhd-brain/

- Shaw, P., Stringaris, A., Nigg, J., & Leibenluft, E. (2023). Evidence of emotion dysregulation as a core symptom of attention-deficit/hyperactivity disorder. *Journal of the American Academy of Child & Adolescent Psychiatry,* 62(1), 58-68. https://doi.org/10.1016/j.jaac.2022.05.023

- Additude. (n.d.). *How to improve executive function skills in ADHD adults.* Retrieved from https://www.additudemag.com/how-to-improve-executive-function-adhd/

- Additude. (n.d.). *The Eisenhower matrix: Prioritizing tasks with ADHD.* Retrieved from https://www.thesummitpsychology.com/blog/the-eisenhower-matrix-prioritizing-tasks-with-adhd

- Tiimo. (n.d.). *Time blocking: ADHD time management technique.* Retrieved from https://www.tiimoapp.com/blog/time-blocking-for-adhders

- Lencioni, S. (2021, June 15). 6 *ways to combat procrastination for adults with ADHD.* Psychology Today. Retrieved from https://www.psychologytoday.com/us/blog/the-best-strategies-for-managing-adult-adhd/202106/6-ways-to-combat-procrastination-for-adults

- Smith, M. (n.d.). *Natural supplements for ADHD symptom relief.* Psych Central. Retrieved from https://psychcentral.com/adhd/adhd-supplements

- Mindful Center. (n.d.). *The digital age dilemma: Navigating ADHD in a hyperconnected world.* Retrieved from https://mindfulcenter.org/the-digital-age-dilemma-navigating-adhd-in-a-hyperconnected-world/

- Additude. (n.d.). *Mind map: Study skills for students with ADHD.* Retrieved from https://www.additudemag.com/mind-map-study-skills-adhd/

- ADHD Centre. (n.d.). 6 *essential mindfulness practices to help with 6 common ADHD symptoms.* Retrieved from https://www.adhdcentre.co.uk/6-essential-mindfulness-practices-to-help-with-6-common-adhd-symptoms/

- La Concierge Psychologist. (n.d.). *How to regulate emotions as an adult with ADHD.* Retrieved from https://laconciergepsychologist.com/

blog/regulate-emotions-adult-adhd/

- Healthline. (n.d.). *How can CBT help with ADHD symptoms?*. Retrieved from https://www.healthline.com/health/adhd/cbt-for-adhd

- HSMH. (n.d.). *Nurturing emotional resilience in children and adults with ADHD: Enhancing mental health and well-being.* Retrieved from https://www.hsmh.co.uk/blog-posts/nurturing-emotional-resilience-in-children-and-adults-with-adhd-enhancing-mental-health-and-well-being

- Just Mind. (n.d.). *Unveiling effective ADHD communication strategies.* Retrieved from https://justmind.org/adhd-communication-strategies/

- ADDA. (n.d.). ADHD *workplace accommodations guide.* Retrieved from https://add.org/adhd-workplace-accommodations-guide/

- ADHD Neuro. (n.d.). *Developing emotional intelligence with ADHD: Your guide to mastering emotions.* Retrieved from https://adhdneuro.com/blog/developing-emotional-intelligence-with-adhd-your-guide-to-mastering-emotions

- CHADD. (n.d.). *CHADD affiliate locator - Find a local ADHD support group.* Retrieved from https://chadd.org/affiliate-locator/

- NCBI. (n.d.). *Eating patterns and dietary interventions in ADHD.* Retrieved from https://www.ncbi.nlm.nih.gov/pmc/articles/

PMC9608000/

- NCBI. (n.d.). *Physical exercise in attention deficit hyperactivity disorder.* Retrieved from https://www.ncbi.nlm.nih.gov/pmc/articles/PMC6945516/

- Sleep Foundation. (n.d.). *ADHD and sleep problems: How are they related?.* Retrieved from https://www.sleepfoundation.org/mental-health/adhd-and-sleep

- Additude. (n.d.). H*ow to get organized with adult ADHD.* Retrieved from https://www.additudemag.com/how-to-get-organized-with-adhd/

- Simcoe Rehab. (n.d.). *ADHD paralysis and the best apps for ADHD 2023.* Retrieved from https://www.simcoerehab.ca/2023/02/17/adhd-paralysis-and-the-best-apps-for-adhd-2023/

- Envision ADHD. (n.d.). *How can technology and apps be leveraged to enhance productivity and organization for adults with ADHD.* Retrieved from https://www.envisionadhd.com/single-post/how-can-technology-and-apps-be-leveraged-to-enhance-productivity-and-organization-for-adults-with-adhd

- Make Use Of. (n.d.). *4 supportive online communities for adults with ADHD.* Retrieved from https://www.makeuseof.com/online-communities-adults-with-adhd/

- Opal. (n.d.). *How Opal helps you manage ADHD and digital distractions.* Retrieved from https://www.opal.so/blog/opal-for-adhd-and-digital-distractions

- Additude. (n.d.). *What is executive function? 7 deficits tied to ADHD.* Retrieved from https://www.additudemag.com/7-executive-function-deficits-linked-to-adhd/

- Additude. (n.d.). *Born this way: Personal stories of life with ADHD.* Retrieved from https://www.additudemag.com/adhd-personal-stories-real-life-people-living-with-adhd/

- One Mind. (2023, November 6). *Unlocking the power of neurodiversity: Embracing ADHD.* Forbes. Retrieved from https://www.forbes.com/sites/onemind/2023/11/06/unlocking-the-power

ABOUT THE AUTHOR

Sharon Banks, a dedicated mother of four from Los Angeles, brings her personal and professional experience to her work. With two children navigating ADHD and autism, Sharon understands the unique challenges of neurodiverse families. For the past 15 years, she has worked closely with children and parents, most recently in special education within schools. Sharon is passionate about equipping the neurodiverse community with practical skills and strategies, aiming to enhance the quality of life for families like hers.

Made in United States
Troutdale, OR
03/11/2025